DINING

IN THE SPIRIT OF NANIBOUJOU

RECIPES COLLECTED FROM
NANIBOUJOU LODGE,
GRAND MARAIS, MINNESOTA

COMPILED AND EDITED BY
BONNIE JEAN SWANSON

Design: Mark Odegard
Photos: Lodge photos by Bob Firth.
Photos: Nature photos by Joanie Campbell

Naniboujou Lodge
20 Naniboujou Trail
Grand Marais, MN 55604

218-387-2688
Naniboujou.com

Front row: Peter, Tim, Jonathan, Paul Ramey, and Tom Rudolph
Back row: Arja, Nancy, Kara, Kristen Ramey, and Heather (Ramey) Rudolph

WELCOME TO THE SPIRIT OF NANIBOUJOU

In April of 1980, we moved with our small family of three children (later that would change to seven children!) to the North Shore of Lake Superior to manage Naniboujou Lodge. Our decision to venture north was largely motivated by our friendship with the former owners, the Wallace family and our familiarity with Naniboujou, and not due to any expertise in managing a lodge.

Later, in 1985, we took a leap of faith and purchased Naniboujou from Christian Corps International. This decision was made prayerfully, as our financial means were not sufficient for such a purchase. God graciously made it very clear that this is where He wanted us and we've been here ever since.

Our intent over many seasons of operation has been to offer a place of quiet respite, and a loving, caring environment exemplifying the love our Heavenly Father has for each of us.

We have been richly blessed with precious staff and guests. We've become family over the years—with Naniboujou as a "place to come home to".

Our prayer for you, whether lodging or dinner guest, sightseer or cookbook reader, is that the true spirit of Naniboujou, Jesus Christ, will touch your life in a rich, refreshing way.

Our heartfelt thanks to all of you.

Tim and Nancy Ramey

TABLE OF CONTENTS

TABLE OF CONTENTS

Proposed club house and grounds at the mouth of the Arrowhead River and overlooking Lake Superior. In the rear is the International Highway, following the shores of Superior for 200 miles from Duluth to Ft. William and Port Arthur, Canada, one of the greatest scenic drives in the world.

The NAN BOUJOU CLUB

Certificate of Founder Membership

FULLY PAID AND NON-ASSESSABLE

NO. 108

THE NANIBOUJOU CLUB

A NON-PROFIT
ORGANIZATION
INCORPORATED

UNDER THE LAWS
OF THE STATE
OF DELAWARE

This is to Certify that

Is a founder member of the Naniboujou Club; that this certificate is issued and accepted subject to the terms and conditions of the Certificate of Incorporation, By-Laws and duly adopted rules and regulations of the Club, by all of which the holder hereof, his heirs, executors, administrators and assigns, agrees to be bound, and may be assigned and transferred only with the consent of the Club and then only after the same has first been offered for sale to the Club and then only to a person elected to membership in the Club and is transferable only on the books of the Club by the holder hereof in person or by duly authorized attorney upon surrender of this certificate properly endorsed.

WITNESS the seal of the corporation and the signatures of its duly authorized officers affixed this _____ day of _____ 1928.

_____
TREASURER, SECRETARY

_____
PRESIDENT

HISTORY OF NANIBOUJOU

Naniboujou, the Cree Indian God of the outdoors, is a powerful, genial, and friendly spirit.

"Naniboujou is why the beaver's tail is flat, why the deer carries a white flag, why the skunk never lets go till he has counted five . . . and why the woodpecker has a splotch of red . . ."

You say a little prayer to Naniboujou, so that he will lead you to game and give safe return from the hunting. You throw a pinch of tobacco in the river to please Naniboujou, so that the fish will come to the hook. You douse the campfire with water before you quit camp, because the woods belong to Naniboujou.

It all began in November of 1927. Seventy-two years ago, the founding members of the Naniboujou Holding Company formed an exclusive club on the northwestern banks of Lake Superior. The club was surrounded by magnificent, densely-forested land providing endless hunting possibilities. The area was filled with bountiful, clear lakes, truly a fisherman's dream. The founders had the right idea. It was their dream, "To live and learn . . . why the raspberry follows the fireweed: . . . the ways of the kingbird . . . and the home life of the beaver."

The Naniboujou Holding Company obtained a 99-year lease for 3,330 acres of land 125 miles northeast of Duluth, Minnesota, along the shores of Lake Superior. The first drawings of the development were shown to the public in March of 1928. This private enterprise had a

THE NANIBOUJOU CLUB
202 PALLADIO BUILDING
DULUTH · MINN ·

January 27, 1928

Helen Wahlstrom,
Ass't. Cashier,
Grand Marais State Bank,
Grand Marais, Minnesota.

Dear Madam:

We are today in receipt of your applicatinn
for Founder Membership in The Naniboujou Club and
your check for one hundred twenty-five dollars in
payment of the membership fee.

We are pleased to inform you that at a
meeting of the Membership Committee this afternoon
you were elected to membership in the Club, and
we enclose your Founder Membership Certificate
herewith.

The Naniboujou Club will offer to its members
every luxury and convenience afforded by the world's
greatest Clubs, and we feel sure that you will
greatly appreciate the appointments and associations
on your trips there.

Very truly yours,

THE NANIBOUJOU CLUB,

By _Jeanette Peterson_
                Secretary.

grand scope. It was to include a large clubhouse with 150 sleeping rooms, a golf course, tennis courts, and a bathing house. Charles F. Kelly, a well known Duluth merchant and President of the company, led the membership drive for 3,300 members. No stock was for sale in this $350,000 – $500,000 development. There would be no promotional advertising. This was to be a private, exclusive club. The 99 year memberships were sold for $200 or more to friends and the friends of friends The desire was for a broad national base of membership. For that reason, and to prevent overcrowding of the facilities, Minnesota residents were limited to 25% of the membership. Just two negative votes by the 24 member board of governors could blackball any prospective member. The prestigious Naniboujou charter members included Babe Ruth, the famous New York Yankee, Jack Dempsey, the former world heavyweight champion, and Ring Lardner, a New York newspaperman.

The original clubhouse included twenty-four guest rooms with a main lodge containing fourteen sets of French doors leading to the outdoors. These doors are still intact, including some of the original canopies. Even some of the lighting in the dining room is original. The largest stone fireplace in the state of Minnesota dominates the west end of the dining room. It was built by a local Swedish stonemason named Carlson out of 200 tons of native rock. Standing some twenty feet high, the fireplace continues to be a showpiece, warming and welcoming the guests of Naniboujou.

Probably the most memorable aspect of the lodge is the wondrously painted 30 x 80 foot dining room. Antoine Goufee, a French artist, painted Cree Indian designs over the walls and the twenty-foot-high domed ceiling (resembling the shape of a canoe). Guests marvel at its originality. "It's straight from an Agatha

Luther, Billy, Luke, Martha, and Suzie Wallace in the mid 1960's.

Christie mystery novel," wrote Tom Clifford in 1972. "The almost psychedelic Cree Indian designs covering the walls and ceiling are like a North Woods answer to the Sistine Chapel." This work of art continually amazes and intrigues, echoing the elegance and style of another era.

1929 marked the opening of the new lodge operated by the newly formed holding company. There was a celebration, with Governor Theodore Christianson christening the lodge on July 7, 1929. This exciting event was followed by abrupt disappointment on November 29 of that same year, Black Friday. The stock market crash spelled disaster for the Naniboujou Company. Even with the help of such distinguished leaders as Honorable George Lead, Mayor of Minneapolis, the Honorable W.I. Nolan, Lt Governor of St. Paul, and L. H. Hill, a capitalist of Albany, Texas, the financial difficulties brought on by the great depression could not be surmounted. By the summer of 1930, everything was turned around. Members quit paying dues and stopped patronizing this northern mecca.

Public participation was needed to keep this large recreational endeavor afloat. In 1932, George Cormack of General Mills in Minneapolis was elected president of the company, but again success was elusive. Credit was eventually shut off following a succession of re-organizations and new management. By 1934, the club was in financial shambles. 1935 brought foreclosures. The only answer seemed to be for a large resort chain to take control.

In 1939, the Arthur Roberts Hotel Chain took over Naniboujou, hiring Mr. Robert MacNab to operate the facility as a hotel. Restoration and some landscaping took place. A great number of recreational activities were added, including archery, croquet, bad-

minton, lawn tennis, trap and skeet shooting, swimming (brr!), and canoeing, as well as indoor Ping-Pong and shuffleboard games. They invested in kitchen equipment and new furnishings for the lodge.

After the death of Arthur Roberts in 1953, the lodge entered another era. Mr. and Mrs. Francis C. Hussey, a local couple, bought the facility. It was now run as a family business—a summer resort and motel for travelers.

Ten years passed, and another change of ownership occurred. Luther and Suzie Wallace left Denver, Colorado, and moved to the north shore of Lake Superior to begin a new life. Their young family, including Martha, age 15, Billy, age 14, and Luke, age 9, would prove to be active participants in the business. Luther, a former chemist and Lieutenant Commander in World War II, with his energetic wife, Suzie, transformed Naniboujou into a family environment founded on Christian principles. Luther welcomed guests at the door with, "Come as you are—glad to have you." Suzie became well known for her wonderful home cooking. Tom Gifford wrote in a 1974 Minneapolis newspaper,"The bread for the sandwiches was homemade and warm, and the tuna salad was made with Russian dressing, and the breeze from the lake rustled in the trees, and the sun shone like a new gold coin hung behind a curtain of faint mist."

As the Wallace boys grew, they handled more of the management of the lodge. But tragedy struck the Wallace family. On September 26, 1977, the young Wallace men, Luke, 23, and Bill, 28, lost their lives when their canoe capsized into Lake Superior at the mouth of the Brule River during a major autumn storm. Suzie and Luther continued to run the lodge for three more years, but in 1980 they sold the business to the Campus Church, a non-denominational Christian church located on the University of Minnesota campus.

This acquisition brought Tim and Nancy Ramey to the North Shore. The Rameys had been working for six years with Fish Enterprises, a Christian project that trained young people in religious fields of work and placed them in vocations around the world. The Rameys accepted a new mission, the management of Naniboujou Lodge. In the autumn of 1980, the Rameys began remodeling the knotty pine wing. The solarium was added in 1983, replacing the outdoor shuffleboard courts. However, within five years the lodge was once again for sale. Tim and Nancy prayed for guidance. With little more than their strong faith and a commitment to serving in whatever direction the Lord provided, Tim and Nancy managed to purchase the lodge with the help of committed friends. Thus began many years of labor, preserving and sensitively renovating the lodge for the pleasure of all who found their way to its open doors.

Soon the lodge was entered on the National Register of Historical Places. Tim and Nancy hired Minneapolis artist Susan Christopherson to begin spreading the Cree Indian designs to the rest of the lodge, including its 80 foot solarium. Both Susan and her husband John took pains to reproduce the original colors from the dining room, as they carefully mixed the modern acrylic latex paints to decorate the rest of the lodge.

Kevin Streeter joined the Rameys as a major staff member in 1985. As head chef for eleven years, it was through Kevin's leadership and creativity that the Naniboujou Lodge developed its strong reputation for fine dining. During the off season, with the lodge closed, Kevin worked side-by-side with Tim on repair work and renovation. Also, as a man of many talents, he coordinated the new

furnishings and designs throughout the lodge rooms and solarium. Kevin's contributions to the lodge were considerable. Although he resigned in 1996, he continues to serve the Rameys in a supportive capacity.

Throughout the Rameys tenure, they have been fortunate to have a number of devoted staff returning year after year. As anyone in business recognizes, this is a great measure of success. I truly believe our guests, both knowingly and unknowingly, enjoy the support of a well seasoned staff. In 1996, I was hired as head chef and immediately recognized the special spirit and camaraderie of Naniboujou. It is a happy and spiritual work environment.

Guests lounge in the comfortable lodge or hike the beautiful Brule River trail in search of the Devils Kettle (a stream of water that mysteriously disappears) high up within a rocky cauldron in the river. They fish the Brule for trout or roam the Lake Superior beach in search of agates. They sit on the Lake's wide shore to glimpse the eagle that perches in his favorite tree, or to watch the Canadian geese trimming the grass. Or like Peter Ramey, a camera buff, many guests love to run outdoors with camera in hand to capture a gloriously full, pink sunset

The dream the founders had for their guests continues in some respects. "Live and learn. Learn why the raspberry follows the fireweed; learn how the fern seed clings to its fronds; learn the ways of the kingbird, the haunts of the woodthrush; learn the pasturage of moose and deer and the home life of the beaver. Swim in the swimming pool, go round 18 holes of golf, or take on a tennis set, come for dinner. Stroll up the trail as far as high falls; walk the beach for agates. Sit and do nothing."

Guests of today do not come for golf or for a dive into a swimming pool; they return seeking a quiet, peaceful, and natural environment. They come to gather their senses and to replenish both body and spirit in a place called Naniboujou.

Naniboujou is open daily to the public from the third week in May until the third week in October. After closing in the autumn and before opening in the spring, we host Elderhostel classes.

Vermillion College in Ely, Minnesota, provides two five-day elderhostel sessions at Naniboujou. The programs are designed to take advantage of the local environment. Studies and activities revolve around topics like local wildflowers, birds, animals, native American culture, artists, dog sledding, etc. Major cleaning and repairs fill November and December.

Since 1985, the lodge has opened its doors for two special evenings of dining and entertainment after Christmas. A 20-foot Christmas tree is decorated to greet the 120 guests each evening. Poinsettias decorate the hall. The massive fireplace glows and warms guests as they enter the hall, leaving behind them a stark, white, winter wonderland. The Ramey family and staff enjoy this event almost as much as the guests, guiding them into the solarium for hot cider to await the arrival of the carolers and an elegant dinner. For many years the Muus family of Grand Marais, with their exceptional musical talent and background, have filled our dining hall with the traditional European carols. The guests dine leisurely and each course gives pause for a song or two. This popular event has become an annual ritual for many of our guests.

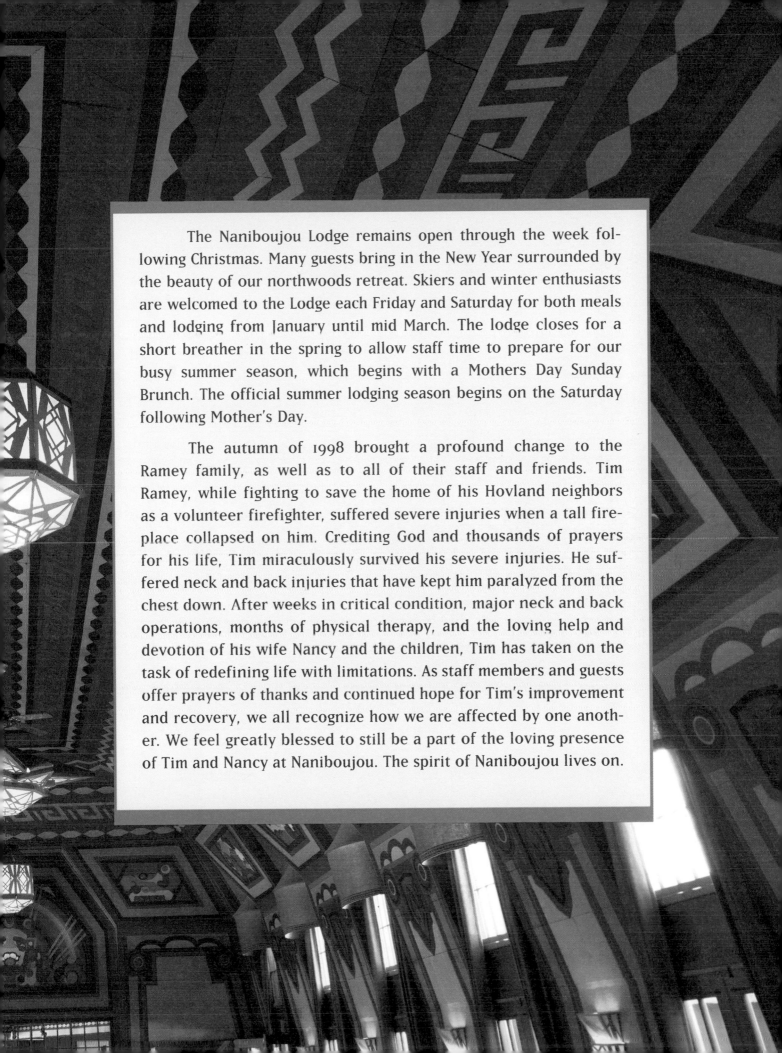

The Naniboujou Lodge remains open through the week following Christmas. Many guests bring in the New Year surrounded by the beauty of our northwoods retreat. Skiers and winter enthusiasts are welcomed to the Lodge each Friday and Saturday for both meals and lodging from January until mid March. The lodge closes for a short breather in the spring to allow staff time to prepare for our busy summer season, which begins with a Mothers Day Sunday Brunch. The official summer lodging season begins on the Saturday following Mother's Day.

The autumn of 1998 brought a profound change to the Ramey family, as well as to all of their staff and friends. Tim Ramey, while fighting to save the home of his Hovland neighbors as a volunteer firefighter, suffered severe injuries when a tall fireplace collapsed on him. Crediting God and thousands of prayers for his life, Tim miraculously survived his severe injuries. He suffered neck and back injuries that have kept him paralyzed from the chest down. After weeks in critical condition, major neck and back operations, months of physical therapy, and the loving help and devotion of his wife Nancy and the children, Tim has taken on the task of redefining life with limitations. As staff members and guests offer prayers of thanks and continued hope for Tim's improvement and recovery, we all recognize how we are affected by one another. We feel greatly blessed to still be a part of the loving presence of Tim and Nancy at Naniboujou. The spirit of Naniboujou lives on.

In the tip of the famous Arrowhead Country

The NANIBOUJOU LODGE

BREAKFAST

BREAKFAST MENUS

THREE BEARS PORRIDGE
WITH CARAMEL OATMEAL TOPPING
BANANA PECAN CHOCOLATE CHIP MUFFINS

EGGS YEMAR
CLARIFIED BUTTER
GOLDEN BREAKFAST BREAD

THE DEMPSEY
BREAKFAST POTATOES
OATMEAL MUFFINS

HOT CHOCOLATE WITH MOCHA CREAM
BLUEBERRY PANCAKES
ORANGE RUM SYRUP

FRUIT SMOOTHIE
WAKE UP HUEVOS
PECAN STICKY MUFFINS

THREE BEARS PORRIDGE

SERVES FOUR.

This is one of our most requested recipes and has appeared recently in the Taste Section of the Minneapolis Star and Tribune. The porridge contains cracked wheat and is cooked with milk, which gives it more depth in flavor and texture. What makes this dish really wonderful is the caramel oat topping, which should be made ahead of time.

PORRIDGE:

3/4 cup	Rolled oats
1/4 cup	Cracked wheat
1/2 tsp	Cinnamon
1/4 tsp	Salt
3 cups	Milk

CARAMEL OAT TOPPING:

4 TB	Butter:
1 cup	Brown sugar
1 tsp	Vanilla
1/4 tsp	Salt
2 cups	Rolled oats
1 cup	Currants, optional

PORRIDGE: In a medium to large saucepan (use a large enough pan, as the oats expand and easily boil over) combine the oats, cracked wheat, cinnamon, salt and milk. Slowly bring to a boil. Immediately reduce to a simmer and partially cover. Cook approximately 8-10 minutes, or until thickened.

CARAMEL OAT TOPPING: Preheat the oven to 325 degrees. In a small saucepan melt the butter over medium low heat. Stir in brown sugar, vanilla and salt. Cook only until the sugar is dissolved. Place the rolled oats in a medium bowl. Pour the hot sugar mixture over oats and mix well. Spread evenly on a lightly oiled baking sheet. Bake 5 minutes, stir, then bake another 5 minutes or until golden brown.

Sprinkle one-half cup of topping over each serving of porridge. Sprinkle with currants, if desired.

Banana Pecan Chocolate Chip Muffins

Makes 1 dozen

A wonderful combination—bananas, nuts, and chocolate. If you have a sweet tooth, or just want something special, try these muffins. Try to pull these from the oven as soon as a tooth pick comes out clean. Muffins dry out so easily and can quickly overbake. Allow to cool about 10 minutes on a rack before removing from tins.

Preheat oven to 325 degrees.

3/4 cup	Butter, melted
1 cup	Sugar
2 large	Eggs
2 cups	Flour
2 tsp	Baking soda
1/2 tsp	Salt
3 TB	Buttermilk
3 large	Bananas, peeled and diced
1 cup	Chopped pecans
3/4 cup	Chocolate chips

In large bowl beat the butter and sugar together. Add the eggs, one at a time, mixing well. In a separate, small bowl, mix the flour, soda and salt together. Gently fold one half of the dry mix into the butter mixture, also gradually adding the buttermilk and bananas. Fold in the remaining one half of the dry mix, along with the pecans and chocolate chips. Do not overmix. Pour batter into greased muffin tins. Filling each muffin cup approximately 2/3 full. Bake for 25 minutes, or until tooth pick comes out clean.

CLARIFIED BUTTER

MAKES APPROXIMATELY 1 1/2 CUPS

In the Nani kitchen we clarify ten pounds of butter at a time. It is used for most of our sauteing and frying. Why butter? There is no substitute for it's flavor, and once clarified, the butter does not easily burn. A little goes a long way. It keeps about 3 weeks in the refrigerator.

1 pound butter, or 4 sticks

Melt the butter over low heat in a small saucepan. Never stir. When completely melted, skim the foam off the top with a large metal spoon. Slowly pour the melted butter into a container. Discard the milky residue remaining in the bottom of the pan. Store clarified butter in the refrigerator.

EGGS YEMAR

SERVES TWO

Not many people realize that the name "Yemar" is Ramey spelled backwards! Our former chef, Kevin Streeter cooked up this name and this dish. It can be prepared so quickly, you will need to have everything ready before hand.

2 TB	Butter	1 cup	Diced tomatoes
2 TB	Scallions	1 cup	Diced cream cheese
6 large	Eggs, mixed well	2 tsp	Chopped chives
			Salt and pepper to taste

Melt the butter in a large skillet. Add scallions and saute a few minutes, or until soft. With a rubber spatula, gently stir in the eggs. Add the tomatoes and cream cheese just as the eggs begin to set. Stir continuously until the cream cheese is melted. Sprinkle with chives and serve immediately.

GOLDEN BREAKFAST BREAD

MAKES 2 LOAVES

Nancy is often in the kitchen on Fridays. I love to watch her work—she is so relaxed. Giant mixers are filled with yeast dough that seems especially happy sitting in the warm baking corner listening to Nancy softly singing. So happy that it periodically slides up and over, causing Nancy, a dish washer, a cook passing by, or anyone, to come over and give it a punch once in a while. By the end of a long day she has mixed, shaped, risen, baked, cooled and wrapped a week's supply of bread and those super duper, huge cinnamon rolls that so many people love. This bread is used for our breakfast toast and for our luncheon turkey sandwich.

3 TB.	Yeast	1/4 tsp	Allspice
1 1/4 cups	Water, 105-115 degrees	1 large	Egg, lightly beaten
3 1/2 TB	Sugar	1/4 cup	Butter, melted
5 1/4 cups	Flour	3/4 cup	Orange juice, warm
1 TB	Salt	1/4 cup	Orange zest (grated peel)
1 tsp	Cinnamon	1 cup	Grated carrots
1/2 tsp	Nutmeg	1 cup	Oat bran
		1/2 cup	Golden raisins

We prepare this bread in a mixer, but it can be prepared by hand also. Dissolve yeast in the warm water. Add the sugar. Slowly mix in the flour, 1 cup at a time, until about half the total flour is incorporated. Mix well. Add the salt, cinnamon, nutmeg, allspice and egg. As you add the rest of the flour, also incorporate the butter, orange juice, zest, carrots, oat bran and raisins. Be sure to only add enough flour to make a firm, yet slightly sticky dough. Too much flour always creates a dry, heavy bread. Knead approximately 10 minutes.

Grease a large bowl and add the dough, flipping over, so oiled side is up. Cover with saran wrap and place the bowl in a draft free, warm spot. Allow the dough to rise until double or approximately 1 1/2 hours. Punch down. Grease two 9" bread loaf pans. Divide dough in half and roll up each half tightly to fit into each pan. Let the dough rise until slightly above the pans, about 50 minutes. Preheat the oven to 375 degrees. Bake for 30-35 minutes, or until golden brown on top. When the bread is done it should be easy to remove from the pan. If it doesn't slide out, bake a little longer.

THE DEMPSEY

SERVES ONE

I presume Jack Dempsey, one of the Charter Members of the Naniboujou Club, would love this wonderful breakfast dish, as do many of our customers. I was considering putting Eggs Benedict back on our menu, but instead came up with this variation. It is so pleasing, probably healthier, different and fun. Our own homemade whole wheat toast serves as a delicious base to this multi-layered entree. Serve with hot breakfast potatoes.

PREHEAT BROILER

2 large	Eggs		2 TB	Lemon juice
1 TB	Butter		2 slices	Whole wheat toast
1/3 cup	Sliced mushrooms		2 slices	Fresh tomato
			2 slices	Havarti cheese, 1 oz each

Fill a large skillet with cold water and bring to a simmer. Add the eggs, keeping the heat low, and cook until set. While the eggs are poaching, in a small skillet over medium heat, add the butter and saute the mushrooms until lightly browned. Add lemon juice to the mushrooms. Remove from heat.

Set the toast on a broiler pan and top each slice with one poached egg. Spread the mushroom mixture on top of each egg and top with a slice of tomato. Broil a few minutes, until warm. Add a cheese slice to the top of each tomato. Broil until the cheese melts.

BREAKFAST POTATOES

SERVES FOUR

Even though this is a simple recipe, it involves some prep time. The potatoes need to be baked before you start this cooking process. (Allow about 40 minutes baking time.) We bake off many pounds of potatoes at a time, cool them down and cut them into 1/2″ chunks. We refrigerate until needed. This started many years ago as a way to use up left over baked potatoes, but now I wouldn't do breakfast potatoes any other way.

3 large	Idaho potatoes
3-4 TB	Clarified Butter
	Salt to taste
3 TB	Basil

Wash potatoes and pierce with a fork. Don't peel. Bake in a 400° oven for approximately 40 minutes or until fork tender. Cool and cut into 1/2″ chunks. Heat the butter in a large skillet until it sizzles. Add the potatoes, salt and basil. Fry over medium high heat, turning often with a spatula until lightly brown and crisp.

Oatmeal Muffins

Makes 18 muffins

Our old worn recipe card gives the Colony Inn credit for these moist muffins. Wherever it came from, it is one of my favorite Naniboujou muffin recipes. Sometimes we add blueberries or raspberries for a nice variation. You will often find this muffin on our Sunday Brunch buffet table.

Preheat oven to 375 degrees.

1 1/2 cups	Oats	1 1/2 cup	Flour
1 1/2 cups	Buttermilk	1 1/2 tsp	Baking soda
3/4 cup	Brown sugar, packed	3/4 tsp	Baking powder
3/4 cup	Corn oil	3/4 tsp	Salt
2 large	Eggs	1 1/4 tsp	Cinnamon
		1/3 cup	Chopped walnuts

In a small bowl, soak the oats in the buttermilk. In a large bowl, beat the brown sugar, oil and eggs together. Stir in the oats and buttermilk. In another small bowl, combine the dry ingredients. Gently mix dry ingredients into oat mixture, mixing as little as possible. Fold in the nuts. Pour batter into greased muffin tins, filling each muffin cup approximately 2/3 full. Bake about 12-15 minutes.

Hot Chocolate with Mocha Whipped Cream

Serves eight

You have to plan ahead for this. Make the mocha whipped cream the day before needed if possible. But, it is rather simple, just use your favorite hot chocolate mix and top it with this creamy, rich chocolate froth for an extra special morning or snack time treat.

1 cup	Heavy cream	1 TB	Sugar
1/2 cup	Chocolate chips	2 tsp	Vanilla
4 tsp	Instant coffee	8 servings	Prepared hot chocolate mix

In small sauce pan heat the cream and chocolate chips over low heat until the chocolate is melted. Add the coffee and sugar, heating until dissolved. Remove from heat. Add the vanilla. Pour the mixture into a bowl, cover and refrigerate at least 4 hours. Whip the chilled mocha just before serving. Pour hot chocolate into each cup and top with a scoop of the mocha cream.

BLUEBERRY PANCAKES

SERVES FOUR TO SIX

Naniboujou is known for its wonderful homemade, fluffy pancakes. This batter may be made ahead and kept in the refrigerator for a few days, but, like anything else, it is best freshly made. Of course, you can add whatever you like: sliced bananas, chopped nuts, or raspberries. Whatever your choice, you are guaranteed a tasty flapjack.

2 large	Eggs	1/4 cup	Sugar
3 cups	Buttermilk	1 TB	Baking powder
1 TB	Butter, melted	2 tsp	Baking soda
3 cups	Flour	1 tsp	Salt
		3 cups	Blueberries

In a large bowl whisk the eggs. Whisk in the buttermilk and butter. In another bowl, mix the remaining ingredients, except the blueberries. Fold these into the egg mixture, mixing as little as possible. It will be lumpy. Heat the griddle until cold water sprinkled on it will bounce around. (It is important to have the griddle hot enough.). Pour about 1/2 cup of batter onto the griddle for each pancake. Sprinkle the blueberries on the top of each pancake. Flip when the center of the pancake bubbles and begins to pop. The second side cooks up quickly. Remove when the bottom is golden brown.

ORANGE RUM SYRUP

MAKES 5 CUPS

This is definitely a favorite at our Sunday Brunch. We are continually asked for the recipe. The kitchen crew is not too keen on grating all the orange zest needed for our gallons of syrup, but at home the task is not so daunting. Carefully avoid grating any of the white pith next to the skin, as it has a bitter taste.

4 cups	Sugar
3 cups	Orange juice
4	Oranges zest, (grated peel)*
1/2 cup	Dark rum

In a medium saucepan combine the sugar, orange juice and orange zest. Stir over low heat until the sugar is dissolved. Bring to a simmer. Remove from the heat. Add the rum and serve.

FRUIT SMOOTHIE

SERVES EIGHT

This refreshing morning pick me up is colorful and even beautiful when served in a tall narrow glass, with a fresh, whole strawberry on top. We prepare large batches, measure them into paper cups, cover and freeze. When ready to serve, we simply microwave for a minute or two and pour into a serving glass. It's a great way to start the day.

4 cups	Strawberries	4 cups	Orange juice
3 cups	Blueberries	3 Bananas, peeled and chopped	

Puree in a blender. You have to do this in small batches. Then mix everything together well. Refrigerate or freeze. Best when served extremely cold.

WAKE UP HUEVOS
SERVES FOUR

I was brave my first year as head chef. I added this dish to our breakfast menu. Maybe it was too different. As the summer season progressed, I realized too few people were ordering it to justify keeping it on the next year's menu. We did get some complaints for removing the huevos from the menu, of course. Here it is for those who did order and enjoyed one of my personal favorites.

3/4 cup	Corn oil	2 cups	Chopped tomatoes
5	Corn tortillas, 1/2" strips	1 1/2 TB	Butter
1/2 cup	Scallions	8 large	Eggs, beaten well
1/2 cup	Julienne red pepper		Salt & pepper to taste
1/4 cup	Chopped jalapeno peppers	4 TB	Sour cream
1 large	Garlic clove, minced	1 cup	Grated cheddar cheese
1 tsp	Ground cumin	1 1/3 cups	Salsa
1 1/2 TB	Chopped cilantro		

STEP ONE:

In a large skillet, heat the oil over medium heat. When the oil is hot, add the tortilla strips. Fry, stirring lightly until golden and crisp. Drain on paper towels. Set aside.

STEP TWO:

Save 2-3 TB of the oil in the skillet and use to saute the scallions, red peppers, jalapeno pepper, and garlic over medium heat just until soft. Stir in the cumin, cilantro, and tomatoes, and cook a few more minutes (not long, as you do not want the tomatoes to get mushy).

STEP THREE:

Melt the butter in a clean large skillet, over medium heat and add the eggs. Stir them with a rubber spatula until soft. Add the vegetable mixture, continue stirring, cooking until the eggs are done. Season with salt and pepper.

To serve: Sprinkle half of the tortilla strips on the bottom of each plate. Top with the eggs and remaining tortilla strips. Top each serving with 1 tablespoon sour cream, 1/4 cup grated cheese and 1/3 cup salsa.

PECAN STICKY MUFFINS

MAKES 1 DOZEN

This is an easy and quick way to create a caramel treat, and may satisfy your sticky caramel roll cravings. As soon as you remove these muffins from the pan, soak the tins in hot water. It will make clean-up so much simpler.

PREHEAT OVEN TO 350 DEGREES.

2 large	Eggs	Topping:	
1/4 cup	Brown sugar	3/4 cup	Melted butter
1 cup	Milk	3/4 cup	Brown sugar
1/4 cup	Butter, melted	3/4 cup	Chopped pecans
1 tsp	Vanilla		
2 cups	Flour		
1 TB	Baking powder		
1 tsp	Cinnamon		
1/4 tsp	Salt		

In a large mixing bowl, beat the eggs, then add the brown sugar, mixing well. Gradually stir in the milk, butter, and vanilla. In a separate bowl combine the flour, baking powder, cinnamon and salt. Gently fold the dry ingredients into the egg mixture. Mix until the flour is incorporated, but do not overmix. There can be some lumps

Measure 1 tablespoon melted butter into each muffin cup, brush to coat the sides, add one tablespoon brown sugar, and tablespoon pecans to each. Spoon 1/4 cup batter on top. Bake approximately 15 minutes, or until light brown and firm center. IMMEDIATELY turn upside down onto flat pan. Remove tin gently.

In the tip of the
famous Arrowhead Country

The
NANIBOUJOU
LODGE

LUNCH

LUNCH MENUS

NORTHERN LIGHT GARDEN SALAD
WITH RASPBERRY POPPY SEED VINAIGRETTE
CHEDDAR CARROT SOUP WITH GINGER

GRILL ROYALE SANDWICH
WITH TOMATO CHUTNEY
HOUSE SALAD
BLUE CHEESE DRESSING

NANIBOUJOU CHICKEN SALAD
FRESH FRUIT
FRENCH BREAD

MULLIGAWNY SOUP
SUPERIOR PASTA SALAD

NORTHERN LIGHT GARDEN SALAD

SERVES FOUR

This is a large beautiful salad. Dark green spinach, red onion slices, bright red strawberries, pure white brie cheese, and the bright raspberry poppyseed vinaigrette. Serve it with good French bread.

8-12 oz	Fresh spinach, washed & dried
1/2	Red onion, thinly sliced
2 cups	Halved fresh strawberries (save 4 whole strawberries)
8 oz	Brie, cut into 12-16 small pieces.
8-12 TB	Raspberry Poppyseed Dressing

Mound the spinach on four medium sized plates. Sprinkle the onion rings and halved strawberries on top. Arrange the brie slices around the edges of the salad. Drizzle the dressing evenly on the salad, and top with a whole strawberry.

RASPBERRY POPPYSEED DRESSING

MAKES 1 CUP

This wonderful, sweet dressing goes so well on our fresh spinach salad, but it is also a frequent choice for our house salad. This recipe comes from the St. Paul Hotel in St. Paul, Minnesota. A note of caution—check your teeth once you finish eating. Those poppy and sesame seeds cling wherever they can. Do use a good quality raspberry vinegar, it makes the world of difference. We use Rothchild raspberry vinegar.

1/2 cup	Sugar	1 tsp	Paprika
1/4 cup	Raspberry vinegar	1 TB	Worcestershire sauce
1/2 cup	Corn oil	1 tsp	Minced onion
2 TB	Poppyseeds		
1 TB	Sesame seeds		

In a small sauce pan whisk the sugar and raspberry vinegar over low heat until the sugar is dissolved. Remove from heat and whisk in the oil. Whisk in the remaining ingredients. Refrigerate until ready to use.

CHEDDAR CARROT SOUP WITH GINGER

SERVES SIX TO EIGHT

Christa is a natural cook. She worked in our kitchen for two summers and then moved on to her first love, training horses. Once in a while she made this marvelous soup and I asked her for the recipe. Well, she never got around to writing it out, partly because she was a natural cook, and improvised as she went along. I was determined to come up with something similar. Here is my version.

2 lbs	Carrots, peeled and cut into 1" chunks	1/2 tsp	Dry ginger
		1/2 tsp	Dry mustard
4 cups	Chicken broth	1/2 tsp	Black pepper
2 TB	Butter	Pinch	Cayenne pepper
2 cups	Chopped onions		Salt, to taste
1/2 cup	Chopped celery	2 cups	Milk
2 cloves	Garlic, minced	1 cup	Cream
1 cup	Half-and-half	1/2 cup	Grated cheddar cheese

In a large saucepan, cook the carrots in the chicken stock until soft. Remove from heat and save both broth and carrots. Melt the butter in a large skillet over low heat and saute the onions, celery and garlic until soft, approximately 5-8 minutes. Add these vegetables, the half-and-half, and all the spices to the carrots and stock. Puree until smooth. Pour the mixture back into the saucepan. Stir in the milk and cream and heat until warm. Add the cheese, and check the seasonings. Mix well and serve once the cheese is melted.

GRILL ROYALE

SERVES SIX

Vegetarians and carnivorous folks alike appreciate this addition to the luncheon menu. The total combination of broiled marinated eggplant and melted Fontina cheese, served on a whole grain bun with spicy tomato chutney makes for quite a tasty sandwich. Cyndy Pawlcyn's *Fog City Diner* cookbook gave me the inspiration for this one.

MARINADED EGGPLANT:

1/4 cup	Soy sauce (Tamari, if possible)
1/2 cup	Olive oil
1-2 cloves	Garlic, minced
1 TB	Grated fresh ginger
1 large	Eggplant, 6 / 1 inch slices
1	Red onion, sliced thin

Mix the soy sauce, olive oil, garlic and ginger in a small bowl. In a a shallow dish, set the sliced eggplant, topping each with a slice of red onion. Pour the marinade over and refrigerate for approximately 1-2 hours.

TOMATO CHUTNEY:

MAKES APPROXIMATELY 2 1/2 CUPS

1 1/2 lbs	Roma tomatoes	3/4 tsp	Cayenne pepper
3/4 cup	Sugar	1/4 cup	Cider vinegar
1 inch piece	Fresh ginger,	3/4 tsp	Salt
	peeled and grated	1/4 cup	Golden raisins
3 cloves	Garlic, minced		

Fill a saucepan large enough to hold the tomatoes with water. Bring to a boil and add the tomatoes. (Have a bowl of ice water ready.) Add the tomatoes to the boiling water and cook about 2 minutes, until the skin looks loose. Immediately drain and put into the ice water. Remove from water and peel. The skins should slide right off the tomatoes. Chop tomatoes coarsely and put into a saucepan with all the remaining ingredients, except for the raisins. Simmer over low heat until thickened. Stir occasionally. Add raisins and cook another 5 minutes.

6 slices	Marinaded eggplant	6 TB	Mayonnaise
6	Kaiser buns	6 slices	Fontina cheese, 1 oz each
6 TB	Tomato chutney		Leaf Lettuce, washed and dried

Place the marinaded eggplant, topped with a slice of red onion on a broiler pan and broil approximately 2 minutes. Flip and broil another 2 minutes, or until soft. Flip back so the onion is on the top. Add the cheese and broil just until melted. Meanwhile, spread one tablespoon tomato chutney on one side of the bun and one tablespoon mayonnaise on the other side, laying leaf lettuce on the top of the mayonnaise. Set an eggplant slice on top of the lettuce and serve.

House Salad

Serves Four

As you may know, the secret to a good salad is fresh, crisp, cold greens and a good dressing. We make all our dressings at Naniboujou. It is really worth the effort.

8 oz	Mixed salad greens	4 TB	Grated Parmesan cheese
2 large	Roma tomatoes, sliced thin	4 TB	Homemade dressing
4 slices	Red onion		

Wash, dry and refrigerate a variety of fresh salad greens. Put about 1 1/2 cups of greens on a small salad plate. Top each salad with a couple wedges of tomato and a thin slice of red onion. Drizzle about 1 tablespoon of dressing over the greens. Sprinkle lightly with Parmesan cheese.

Blue Cheese Dressing

Makes about 3 cups

We recently added this dressing because of many customer requests. This is good and couldn't be easier. One of my favorite afternoon snacks is a slice of french bread dipped into a spoonful of this lovely dressing.

6 oz	Crumbled blue cheese	2 tsp	Worcestershire sauce
1 cup	Mayonnaise	2 tsp	Minced garlic
1/2 cup	Sour cream	3/4 tsp	Salt
1/4 cup	Buttermilk	3/4 tsp	Pepper

Simply mix all the ingredients together in a large bowl. Add more buttermilk if it seems too thick.

NANIBOUJOU CHICKEN SALAD

SERVES FOUR

This luncheon entree is an old standby, one we definitely cannot remove from the menu. Our customers love this salad. But then again, we serve quite a tasty chicken salad. For one thing, we poach the chicken breasts, which keeps the meat moist. A dash of garlic powder and thyme along with the traditional ingredients seems to satisfy the appetites of both young and old.

1 1/2 lbs	Chicken breasts, skinless and boneless	3/4 tsp	Garlic powder
		3/4 tsp	Dried thyme
2 ribs	Celery, finely chopped		Salt and pepper to taste
1 cup	Seedless red grapes	3/4-1 cup	Mayonnaise
		1/4 cup	Toasted almonds

Bring a medium sized pan of water to a boil. Add the chicken breasts, and when the water returns to a boil turn the heat off. Leave the chicken in the hot water for about 25 minutes, or until cooked through. Remove and cut into 1-inch chunks. Add the celery, grapes, garlic powder, thyme, salt, pepper, and mayonnaise. Sprinkle a tablespoon of almonds on the top of each serving.

FRENCH BREAD

MAKES 2 LOAVES

I bake about 32 baguettes at a time at the lodge. Sometimes twice a day. People in the kitchen get tired of me propping loaves of bread here and there to rise, but they love the samples I give them. Sometimes tired and weary I exclaim, "I may stop baking our own french bread!" Alarmed at the thought, Lisa, a waitress and avid fan, quickly would head for the dining room to take a poll of her diners. Returning to the kitchen, Lisa claimed her diners said, "Keep the fresh bread coming, it's definitely worth the labor." So—I carry on. This is a basic french bread recipe. The key to a good loaf is to be sure to add enough salt, and not too much flour. Knead the dough a good long time.

2 TB	Yeast	1 TB	Salt
2 1/2 cups	Warm water, 110 to 150 degrees	1/2 cup	Cold water
6-7 cups	Flour	1 1/2 tsp	Salt

Mix the yeast into the water until dissolved. Wait about 10 minutes to see if yeast bubbles. If it doesn't bubble the yeast is not good. Add 4 cups of the flour and the salt. Mix well. Gradually add the remaining flour, mixing as you add. Some days you will need more flour, some days less, depending on the humidity. Add enough to form soft ball that leaves the sides of the bowl. Knead at least 10 minutes.

Place the dough in a large buttered bowl. Turn the dough over and cover with plastic wrap. Set it in a warm area away from drafts. Let it rise until doubled, 1 to 1 1/2 hours. If time allows punch dough and let rise a second time. Divide the dough into two. Preheat the oven to 375° Pat or roll each ball of dough into the length of your pan, then roll it tightly to form each loaf, pinching the edges together. Set seam side down into greased french bread pan, that is lightly coated with corn meal. Mix the cold water and salt together and brush onto the top of each loaf. Let rise until it rises a little above the pan. Again brush with salt water. Put into HOT oven and bake about 35-45 minutes, or until dark golden brown.

MULLIGATAWNY SOUP

SERVES SIX TO EIGHT

I have found so many recipes for this East Indian soup. If you have never tasted it, you are in for a very pleasant surprise. Sometimes we have difficulty explaining this soup to our customers. It all sounds so strange. They ask, "What's in the soup?" "Lots of diced vegetables, apples, rice, chicken and curry." It sounds strange, but, if you like curry, I think you will enjoy this soup. We have a few customers so fond of this soup that they will call ahead to find out when we will be serving Mulligatawny.

1 large	Eggplant, diced (about 2 cups)	2	Granny Smith apples, diced
1/4 cup	Butter	2 1/2 tsp	Curry powder
2 cups	Finely diced onion		Salt, to taste
1/2 cup	Finely diced celery	1/2 tsp	White pepper
1 cup	Flour	1/2 cup	Cooked rice
10 cups	Chicken stock	2 oz	Chicken, cooked, cut 1" pcs.
1/2 cup	Diced green pepper	2 cups	Milk
		1 cup	Cream

Fill a medium size kettle with water and bring to a boil. Add the eggplant, turning heat to low, and blanch for 5 minutes. Remove from heat and drain. In a large kettle, melt the butter and saute the onion and celery until soft. Add the flour, whisking until it is incorporated and the flour is cooked (approximately 2 minutes). Continue whisking, slowly adding the chicken stock. Add the eggplant, green pepper and apple. Cook for 5-10 minutes on low heat. Add the curry, salt, pepper, rice, chicken, milk and cream. Keep heating on low until hot. Never boil. Serve hot.

SUPERIOR PASTA SALAD

SERVES EIGHT

An easy salad, and quite flavorful. Try to serve it the day you prepare it, as within a day or two the mushrooms become slightly discolored. It is pretty served on a bed of fresh spinach greens.

8 oz	Bacon
12 oz	Pasta, nuggets
2 cups	Mayonnaise
1/2 cup	Buttermilk
2 TB	Lemon juice
2 TB	Dijon mustard
1 TB	Sugar
1 lbs	Fresh mushrooms, sliced
10 oz	Frozen peas, thawed
	Fresh spinach - optional
	Fresh tomatoes - wedges optional

In a large skillet, saute the bacon until crisp. Set on paper towels to cool, then chop coarsely. Fill a 4 quart kettle with water and when it comes to a boil add the pasta and a little salt. Cook, stirring occasionally, until tender, about 6-8 minutes. Drain the pasta and rinse in cold water. Chill. In a large bowl, whisk the mayonnaise, buttermilk, lemon juice, mustard and sugar together. Add the chilled pasta, bacon pieces, mushrooms and peas. Season with salt and pepper.

We plate this salad on a bed of fresh spinach leaves with tomato wedges on the side.

In the tip of the
famous Arrowhead Country

The
NANIBOUJOU
LODGE

DINNER

DINNER MENUS

SHERRIED WILD RICE SOUP

SAUTEED WALLEYE *with* ALMOND CRUST

GARLIC ROASTED POTATOES

FRENCH GLAZED CARROTS

DANISH CREME/RASPBERRY SAUCE

RIB-EYE STEAK *with* BALSAMIC GLAZE

and MUSHROOM TOAST

BAKED BUTTERNUT SQUASH

FRENCH POTATO PANCAKES

WHITE CHOCOLATE MOUSSE

SPINACH BASIL SOUP *with* LEMON

PADDLERS PASTA

DECADENT ALMOND CHEESECAKE

HOUSE SALAD

with HONEY DIJON DRESSING

PORK TENDERLOIN

with CRANBERRY WINE SAUCE

SAVORY PARMESAN GREEN BEANS

WILD RICE/BASMATI PILAF

CHOCOLATE TORTE

WHITE BEAN SOUP *with* SAUSAGE

CHICKEN CUTLET PARMESAN

and CHUNKY TOMATO SAUCE

GARLIC MASHED POTATOES

SWEET CORN WITH PEPPERS

RHUBARB COBBLER

CREAM CHEESE TOMATO SOUP

VEGETARIAN SHEPHERD'S PIE

PICKLED BEETS

CRANBERRY PUDDING

SHERRIED WILD RICE SOUP

SERVES SIX TO EIGHT

Our guests come up to the north woods expecting both fresh fish and wild rice soup. This soup recipe could have many variations. For instance, if desired, you could substitute chicken for the ham, or you could add other vegetables. You will need about 1 cup raw wild rice to get 3 cups of cooked rice. This soup goes together rather quickly. It is definitely tastier if you let it sit a day, allowing the flavors to develop or "marry", as the French would say. Use more rice, if you like a thicker soup.

4 TB	Butter	3 cups	Cooked wild rice*
3/4 cup	Chopped onions	4 oz	Ham, diced
3/4 cup	Chopped celery	2 cups	Half and half
8 oz	Fresh mushrooms, chopped	1/4 cup	Sherry
6 cups	Chicken broth	Salt and pepper to taste	
1 /2 cup	Diced carrots	1 tsp	Dried thyme

In a large saucepan, saute the onions, celery, and mushrooms in butter. Add the chicken broth, carrots, wild rice, and ham. Bring to a boil, lower heat and simmer for about 20 minutes. Add remaining ingredients and heat until hot.

*To cook wild rice: Put 1 cup of wild rice in a medium saucepan and cover with 3-4 inches or more of water. Do not cover. Bring to a boil, lower heat and simmer approximately 30-40 minutes, adding more water if necessary. Cook until the rice is tender. Drain.

SAUTEED WALLEYE WITH SEASONED ALMOND CRUST

SERVES SIX

Personally, I love food with texture. Some years we have served walleye with this crunchy crust that I discovered from *Cafe Brenda's* cookbook, making a few revisions of my own. The walleye stays moist and soft inside the golden brown almond crust. Serve with a few wedges of lemon.

2 cups	Flour	2 cups	Ground almonds
1 1/2 tsp	Salt	2	Lemons, zest only
1/4 tsp	Cayenne pepper	6 /6 oz	Skinless walleye fillets
1/4 tsp	Lemon pepper	4-6 TB	Clarified butter
3 large	Eggs		(See page 35)

You will need three large plates to prepare the toppings. In the first plate, mix the flour, salt, cayenne and lemon pepper with a fork until well blended. Whisk the eggs in the second plate. In the third plate, mix the almonds and grated lemon peel together. Dip each fillet on both sides first into the flour mixture, then the eggs, and finally into the almond mix. You can do this ahead of time. Simply cover the coated fillets with plastic wrap and refrigerate until ready to saute.

Divide the clarified butter between two large skillets over high heat. When butter sizzles, add the fillets, immediately turning the heat to medium-low.

Cook approximately 4-6 minutes on each side, depending on thickness of the fillets. The almond crust should be golden brown. Serve immediately.

GARLIC ROASTED POTATOES

SERVES SIX

This dish is a nice, simple potato variation. Do be generous with the garlic.

PREHEAT THE OVEN TO 400 DEGREES.

5-6	Idaho potatoes
1/4 cup	Olive oil
6-8 cloves	Garlic, peeled and minced
	Salt to taste

Wash, but do not peel the potatoes. Cut each potato into about 8 chunks. Spread out on a cookie sheet. Drizzle with olive oil and garlic. Using a fork, stir and mix the potatoes, olive oil and garlic together. Bake approximately 15- 20 minutes, or until tender and golden brown. Sprinkle with salt and serve.

FRENCH GLAZED CARROTS

SERVES SIX TO EIGHT

4 cups	Sliced carrots, cut in 1" diagonal slices
4 TB	Butter
5 TB	Brown sugar
1/2 cup	Orange juice
1 tsp	Ground ginger

Fill a medium saucepan with salted water. Bring to a boil over high heat. Add carrots and cook until almost fork tender. Drain. In a medium-sized skillet, melt the butter and add the brown sugar and orange juice. Bring to a boil and add the ginger, boiling about 5 minutes. Add the cooked carrots, simmer until sauce somewhat thickens and the carrots are fully cooked. Serve.

DANISH CREME WITH RASPBERRY SAUCE

SERVES EIGHT

This recipe alone may sell this cook book. So many people have asked, and even tried to negotiate for a copy. For instance, one afternoon I received a phone call from a local art gallery. Apparently they had a disgruntled customer who claimed they would be able to make amends with him, if somehow, they could glean the Danish Creme recipe from the Naniboujou Lodge.

This is a rich dessert, yet it is served in small portions. Top it with raspberry sauce and a dab of whipped cream.

2 envelopes	Plain gelatin	1 3/4 cup	Heavy cream
6 TB	Cold water	16 oz	Sour cream
3/4 cup	Half and half		Raspberry sauce
1 3/4 cup	Sugar		*(recipe follows)*
			Whipped cream

In a small bowl, sprinkle the gelatin over the water. Let it sit for a few minutes. Place in the microwave for approximately 1 minute. Stir to dissolve.

In a small saucepan, mix the half and half, sugar, and cream. Heat just to warm. Pour into a large bowl. Add the sour cream and mix together until smooth. Mix in the gelatin and stir until smooth and mixed well.

Pour into eight small serving dishes. Portion size is about 2/3 of a cup. (We use stemmed glass sherbet dishes.) Refrigerate until firm. Top with 1/2 cup raspberry sauce, and a dollop of whipped cream.

RASPBERRY SAUCE

1 pkg	Junket Danish dessert mix
2 1/2 cups	Water
10 oz	Frozen whole raspberries, thawed

In a small saucepan mix the junket and water together. Heat to a boil. Boil for one minute. Remove from the heat and let cool slightly. Add the raspberries, mixing well. Refrigerate.

SPINACH BASIL SOUP WITH LEMON

SERVES SIX TO EIGHT

This soup was a previous hit in my own two restaurants, and it is again a favorite at the Naniboujou. After so many requests, this recipe is in print. It is a thick, flavorful soup. Lemon seems to give it the right kick. It is so easy, some people may wonder what all the fuss is about. Indulge, here it is.

6 TB	Butter
1 1/2 cups	Finely chopped onion
1 clove	Garlic, peeled and minced
16 oz	Frozen chopped spinach, thawed and drained
1 TB	Dried basil
3 cups	Chicken broth
1/2 cup	Grated Parmesan cheese
1 cup	Heavy cream
2 tsp	Salt
2 tsp	Lemon juice
1/2 tsp	Pepper
1/4 tsp	Lemon zest,(grated peel)

In a large saucepan, melt the butter over low heat and saute the onion until soft, about 10 minutes. Add the garlic. sauteing another minute or two. Mix in the drained spinach, basil and chicken broth and bring to a boil. Reduce the heat and simmer, uncovered, approximately 10 minutes. Mix in the remaining ingredients. Heat and serve. Voila!

Paddlers Pasta

Serves Four to Six

A colorful vegetarian dish. This flavorful dish gets its sparkle from the combination of tangy artichokes and a wonderful pesto. For the pasta, we use a multi-colored spiral shape. It is a breeze to make. The toasted pine nuts complement this entree.

1 cup	Finely diced onions
3 TB	Clarified butter
1 cup	Finely diced onions
1 cup	Chopped, fresh tomatoes
6 large	Canned artichoke hearts, drained and quartered
1 lb	Dry pasta spirals, cooked
1 cup	Pesto
1/3 cup	Grated Parmesan cheese
1/2 cup	Pinenuts, toasted

In a large saucepan over medium heat, saute the onions in butter until soft. Add the tomatoes and artichoke hearts, heating until warm. Add pasta and pesto continually mixing so the mixture does not stick to the bottom of the pan. Heat until hot. Serve sprinkled with Parmesan cheese and pinenuts.

NANIBOUJOU CHEESECAKES

As Naniboujou's dessert baker for several years, Marcia Stoub is a cheesecake whiz, continually devising new variations to tantalize not only our customers, but also the staff. Sampling is imperative in a restaurant's kitchen. We want our staff to understand and appreciate the quality of the food they are serving. When Marcia tries something new, we all clamor about her with forks in hand.

Some general instructions regarding cheesecake may be helpful, as we all know cheesecake can be a tricky business. First of all, the ingredients should be at room temperature. Always mix the ingredients at the lowest speed on your mixer, and beat only until eggs and flavorings are blended. Overbeating can incorporate too much air into the batter, which causes a cheesecake to puff and fall, creating cracks. Place a shallow pan half full of water on the bottom oven rack, below the cheesecake. This helps keep the surface moist. Bake at 325 degrees for 60-75 minutes. To determine if a cheesecake is done, gently shake the pan. If the center jiggles only slightly and the cheesecake looks nearly set, it is done. The center will firm up as it cools. Cool the cheesecake out of reach of any draft. After the cake has cooled for 10 minutes remove the sides of the pan. This will prevent the cake from cracking as it cools.

CRUST:		BASIC CHEESECAKE	
1 1/2 cups	Graham cracker crumbs	32 oz	Cream cheese
1/3 cup	Melted butter	1 3/4 cups	Sugar
1/3 cup	Sugar	1/8 tsp	Salt
TOPPING:		5 large	Eggs
2 cups	Sour cream	1 1/4 tsp	Vanilla
1/2 cup	Sugar		
1 1/2 tsp	Vanilla		

CRUST: In a small bowl combine the crumbs, butter and sugar, and press the mixture into the bottom of a 9" spring form pan.

CHEESECAKE: In a mixing bowl beat the cream cheese, sugar and salt together. Add the eggs, one at a time, beating until very smooth. Mix in the vanilla. Pour this mixture onto the crust. Bake at 350 degrees for 1 hour and 10 minutes, or until done. Remove from the oven and turn the oven up to 400 degrees. Cool the cake for 10 minutes.

TOPPING: Mix the topping ingredients together and pour onto the cooled cake. Return to the oven for 10 minutes or more. Cool completely, then remove from the pan. Refrigerate for 3 hours before serving. Can be frozen.

DECADENT ALMOND CHEESECAKE

SERVES TWELVE TO SIXTEEN

PREHEAT OVEN TO 350 DEGREES.

1 cup	Almonds, toasted & ground*	5 large	Eggs
2 TB	Butter, melted	1/4 cup	Amaretto
4/8 oz pkgs	Cream cheese	2/3 cup	Chopped almonds, toasted*
1 1/4 cup	Sugar	1 cup	Whipping cream
2 tsp	Vanilla	2 TB	Amaretto
1/2 tsp	Almond extract		

Mix the almonds and butter together in a small bowl. Press this mixture into the bottom of a 9 inch springform pan. In a large mixing bowl, beat the cream cheese, sugar, vanilla and almond extract until fluffy. Add the eggs, one at a time, beating on low speed until combined. Stir in the Amaretto and almonds. Pour this mixture on top of the crust. Bake for approximately 70 minutes. Cool on a wire rack for 15 minutes, then loosen the sides of the pan. Continue cooling for 30 minutes more. Remove the sides of the pan. Cool. Chill at least 4 hours.

Whip the cream until peaks form, add the Amaretto. Serve a small dollop on each slice of cheesecake.

* Heat a skillet. Add almonds and stir continuously until lightly browned.

WHITE BEAN SOUP WITH SAUSAGE

SERVES SIX TO EIGHT

In a restaurant kitchen, as well as at home, it makes sense to make use of leftovers. Turkey wild rice sausage accumulates in our kitchen, as every morning, including Sunday brunch, we prebake sausage. We do freeze leftovers and use them in our brunch baked dishes. But one day I recalled a wonderful white bean soup recipe that called for chorizo sausage. I substituted the turkey wild rice sausage, and it turned out a winner.

2 TB	Butter
1 1/2 cups	Chopped onions
2 stalks	Celery, chopped
2 cloves	Garlic, minced
3/4 lb	Ham, cut into 1/2 inch cubes
2 cups	Diced potatoes
1 cup	Diced carrots
2 qts	Water
3/4 lb	Sausage, diced (chorizo or turkey)
10 oz	Frozen spinach, thawed and drained
2 (15 oz cans)	White beans, drained
2 tsp	Salt
1/2 tsp	Pepper

Melt the butter in a 4 quart saucepan and sauté the onions, celery and garlic over low heat for about 10 minutes, or until soft. Add the ham and sauté another 5 minutes. In a medium size saucepan, cover the potatoes and carrots with the water and bring to a boil. Lower heat and simmer for 20 minutes, or until fork tender. Do not drain. Add the sauteed vegetables, ham, sausage and spinach. Cook 10-15 minutes. Add the white beans, salt and pepper and additional water, if necessary. Heat, and serve.

CHICKEN CUTLET PARMESAN
WITH CHUNKY TOMATO SAUCE

SERVES EIGHT

A six ounce chicken breast flattened and coated with a Parmesan bread crust will fill up your fry pan, and your stomach. The simple sweet and sour tomato sauce is a nice accompaniment. This entree can also be prepped ahead of time, covered with plastic wrap, and refrigerated until ready to sauté.

8 /6 oz	Chicken breasts, boneless and skinless
1 1/2 cups	Flour
4 tsp	Salt
2 tsp	Pepper
6 large	Eggs, well beaten
4 TB	Cream
1 1/2 cups	Grated Parmesan cheese
1 1/2 cups	Fresh bread crumbs
1/4 cup	Olive oil
	Chunky tomato sauce

Place each chicken breast between plastic wrap and flatten cutlet by pounding with a meat mallet until about 1/4 inch thick. Using 3 flat dishes, combine flour, salt and pepper in one, the eggs and cream beaten together in another, and the Parmesan cheese and bread crumbs in the third. Dip both sides of each chicken fillet first into the flour mixture, then into the egg mixture, and lastly into the cheese crumb mixture. Cover with plastic wrap and refrigerate until needed.

Heat the 2 tablespoons olive oil in each of 2 large skillets. When the oil is hot, add two cutlets to each skillet. Lower heat to medium low. Sauté the chicken, turning when the bottom looks golden brown, or in approximately 4 minutes. Sauté for another 3-4 minutes, or until golden brown on both sides. Set in a warm oven while preparing the second batch. Serve with 1/2 cup of the Chunky Tomato Sauce on the side.

CHUNKY TOMATO SAUCE

SERVES EIGHT

2 TB	Butter
2 TB	Diced green peppers
2 TB	Flour
2 14oz cans	Diced tomatoes
2 TB	Cider vinegar
2 TB	Sugar
1 tsp	Dried tarragon

In a small saucepan, heat the butter and saute the green peppers until tender (just a minute or two). Add the flour, stirring continually with a fork for a minute, or until the flour is cooked. Add the tomatoes, juice and all, the vinegar, sugar and tarragon. Cook, stirring continually, until everything is mixed well, and slightly thickened. Serve hot, on the side of the cutlet.

GARLIC MASHED POTATOES

SERVES EIGHT

The secret to fluffy, tasty mashed potatoes is to not overcook the potatoes. You don't want the flavor to end up in the water you throw away. Also, always add the salt to the water when cooking. Whip the potatoes well with hot milk and butter.

6-8	Idaho potatoes, peeled and cut into 2 inch pieces
1 TB	Salt
5	Garlic cloves, whole, skin removed
1/4 cup	Butter, melted
1/3 cup	Milk, heated

In a large saucepan cover the potatoes with water, add salt and garlic cloves and bring to a boil. Lower heat and simmer for approximately 20 minutes, or until fork tender. Drain. Mash the potatoes and garlic cloves with the butter and milk, until fluffy.

SWEET CORN WITH PEPPERS

SERVES EIGHT

Yellow corn with bright red and green peppers looks and tastes great. Cumin gives it that interesting flavor.

1/3 cup	Chopped Onions	1 1/2 lb	Frozen corn
1/3 cup	Diced red pepper	2 tsp	Ground cumin
1/3 cup	Diced green pepper	Salt to taste	
2 TB	Butter		

In a medium skillet, saute the onions and peppers in the butter. In a medium saucepan, heat the corn in a little water until hot. Drain. Add the sauteed vegetables. Mix in the cumin and salt. Serve.

RHUBARB COBBLER

SERVES EIGHT

Cobblers are so versatile. Whenever Marcia bakes a batch, they disappear. This is one of my own favorite cobbler recipes. The crunch of the pecans and the cinnamon-orange flavor are wonderful.

PREHEAT THE OVEN TO 400 DEGREES.

1 cup	Sugar	1/3 cup	Sugar
2 TB	Cornstarch	1 1/2 tsp	Baking powder
1 tsp	Cinnamon	1/2 tsp	Salt
4 cups	Chopped rhubarb, 1" pieces	1/2 cup	Milk
1 TB	Water	1/2 cup	Chopped pecans
6 TB	Butter, cold	1 tsp	Grated orange peel
1 cup	Flour		

In a medium saucepan, combine the sugar, cornstarch and cinnamon together. Add the rhubarb, water, and 2 tablespoons of the butter and bring to a boil. Boil for one minute. Pour while hot into a 8 x 8 inch baking dish. Set this in the oven to keep it hot. Meanwhile, mix the flour, sugar, baking powder and salt together. Cut the remaining 4 tablespoons butter into the dry ingredients. Gently mix in the milk, pecans and orange peel. Drop by spoonfuls onto the hot rhubarb. Bake for approximately 20 minutes, or until golden brown and bubbly.

Rib Eye Steak With Balsamic Glaze and Mushroom Toast

Serves Four

We prepare this steak bistro-style. No oil is used, only an extremely hot cast-iron fry pan. The pan should be so hot that when salt is sprinkled on the pan, it will dance around. This hot heat method seals in the juices.

	Salt
4 /10 oz	Rib Eye Steaks, 1/2 inch thick

Glaze:

4 TB	Butter, soft
4 TB	Balsamic vinegar
2 TB	Finely chopped shallots
8 slices	Mushroom Toast

Heat two large cast iron fry pans until very hot. Sprinkle with a little salt. Add two steaks to each pan. Keep heat on high. Fry for 4-5 minutes. Turn and fry another 3-4 minutes for rare, 5-6 minutes for medium and 7-8 minutes for well done. Remove steaks to warm plates. Turn heat off and add half the butter, shallots and vinegar to each pan. Stir constantly for a few minutes until the shallots are cooked. Pour glaze over the top of each steak. Serve with 2 slices of Mushroom Toast.

MUSHROOM TOAST

MAKES 1 1/2 CUPS

Cindy Pawclyn, from the *Fog City Diner* in San Francisco (and cookbook of the same name), demonstrated this recipe for a cooking class I attended. When we decided to serve the rib eye steak at Naniboujou, I thought it would make a great accompaniment. It is time-consuming to make, but then most good things are. If you want your house to smell like you are an accomplished chef, simmer a batch of this and invite the neighbors in for a smell and a taste.

2	Shallots, minced	1/2 cup	Chicken stock,
4 TB	Butter	1 cup	Heavy cream
3/4 lb	Mushrooms, chopped	1/4 tsp	Salt
3/4 tsp	Dried thyme	1/8 tsp	Pepper
1 1/4 cups	White dry wine	Dash	Nutmeg

FOR CROUTONS:
8 slices   1/2" thick slices of French bread cut at an angle, lightly toasted,

Sauté the shallots in butter in a large skillet over low heat, until tender. Add the mushrooms and sauté 5 minutes more. Add thyme and white wine, turning the heat to medium high. Reduce the liquid until it almost evaporates (about 10 minutes). Add the chicken stock and again bring to a boil. Lower heat to medium and reduce this mixture by half. Stir in the cream and seasonings. Cook until thickened, approximately 15-20 minutes. The mixture should coat the back of a spoon. Refrigerate until needed.

TO SERVE: Spread about 1 tablespoon of the mushroom mixture onto each crouton and set under broiler until hot.

BAKED BUTTERNUT SQUASH

SERVES FOUR

So easy, and a fine color and taste. I have never understood why more restaurants do not serve this vegetable. We often serve it, especially to groups. One evening we served this to a chef at his groom's dinner. He commented he had never thought of serving squash in his restaurant, and he found it quite appealing. The only difficulty in the recipe is cutting the squash, be careful of your fingers.

PREHEAT OVEN TO 350 DEGREES.

1 large	Butternut squash
4 TB	Butter, melted
1 1/2 tsp	Nutmeg

Cut squash into quarters. Follow the ridges for easier cutting. Remove the seeds. Set each piece with the cut side up on a flat cooking sheet or baking dish. Put 1 tablespoon butter on each piece. Sprinkle with grated nutmeg. Bake approximately 25 minutes, or until fork tender.

FRENCH POTATO PANCAKES

SERVES FOUR TO SIX

Looking for a way to use up left over mashed potatoes? I often serve this on Sunday evenings at the lodge. It is a homey, comfort dish.

BUTTER AN 8″ X 12″ BAKING DISH.

3	Egg yolks
4 cups	Mashed potatoes
4 TB	Butter, melted
1 1/2 tsp	Dried tarragon
1 TB	Minced fresh parsley
1 1/2 tsp	Salt
3/4 tsp	Black pepper
1/2 tsp	Ground nutmeg
1/4 cup	Flour
1/4 cup	Minced parsley

In a large bowl, mix the egg yolks and add the potatoes, mixing well. Add 2 tablespoons of the butter and all of the herbs and seasonings. Add the flour and parsley, mixing well. Spread into the prepared baking dish and refrigerate at least half an hour. Preheat the oven to 375°. Just before baking, spread the remaining 2 tablespoons butter on the top. Sprinkle with a little more minced parsley, if desired. Bake approximately 20-25 minutes, or until golden brown. Cut into squares and serve.

WHITE CHOCOLATE MOUSSE

SERVES TWELVE TO SIXTEEN

Whenever possible buy the best quality chocolate. It does make a difference. We try to use Belgian chocolate because of its great flavor and smooth consistency. This is a rich dessert, so cut the slices small.

1 1/4 cups	Oreo cookie crumbs
1/2 cup	Butter, melted
8 oz	Semi-sweet chocolate
3 3/4 cups	Heavy cream, divided
12 oz	White chocolate
1 TB	Plain gelatin
1/4 cup	Cold water

In a small bowl, mix the cookie crumbs with the butter and press into the bottom of an 8 inch springform pan. In a double boiler, stir and melt the semi-sweet chocolate with 3/4 cup of cream. Pour the mixture on top of the crust and freeze.

Meanwhile, in a double boiler, melt the white chocolate with 1 cup of cream stirring often, as white chocolate burns easily. Remove from heat. In a small bowl sprinkle the gelatin over the cold water and mix with a fork. Let it stand for 3 minutes, then microwave it for 2 minutes, or until the gelatin is dissolved. Stir the gelatin into the white chocolate mixture. Pour this mixture into a large, clean bowl and allow it to sit until cool and thick.

In a large mixing bowl, beat the remaining 2 cups of cream until it holds peaks. Gently fold the whipped cream (in small amounts) into the cooled white chocolate mixture. Pour onto the frozen crust. Refrigerate until ready to serve.

HONEY DIJON DRESSING

MAKES 3 CUPS

This has been a popular dressing at the Naniboujou for several years. It has a nice tangy flavor. Make it a day ahead, or at least a few hours ahead, for the flavors to develop.

1 cup	Mayonnaise
1 cup	Plain yogurt
1/2 cup	Honey mustard
1/2 cup	Balsamic vinegar
2 TB	Finely chopped onions
1 1/2 tsp	Dried tarragon
1/2 tsp	Dried basil
1/8 tsp	Black pepper

Mix the mayonnaise, yogurt and honey mustard together in a bowl. Add the vinegar, onion and seasonings and mix well. Refrigerate until ready to use.

Pork Tenderloin With Cranberry Wine Sauce

Serves Eight

Kevin Streeter, our former chef, introduced this recipe to Naniboujou, and our customers are eternally grateful. It is one of our most popular entrees. The pork is marinated, then broiled and served on top of the lovely cranberry wine sauce.

Pork marinade:

2 cups	Soy sauce
1 cup	Brown sugar
3 cloves	Garlic, peeled and minced
1 TB	Fresh ginger, minced
1 tsp	Black pepper
2 lbs	Pork tenderloin, 1 oz pieces

Cranberry wine sauce:

1/2 cup +2 TB	Butter, room temperature
15 oz	Cranberries
1/2 cup	Finely diced onions
1 cube	Chicken bouillon
1 1/2 cups	Burgundy wine (or dry red wine)
1 cup+2TB	Sugar

Pork marinade: In a large bowl, mix all of the ingredients together. Add the pork and marinate overnight, or at least 2 hours.

Cranberry wine sauce: Use a medium size stainless steel pan, not aluminum. Melt 2 tablespoons of butter, add the cranberries and onion and sauté over medium low heat until the cranberries pop. Turn the heat to a simmer and add the chicken bouillon cube, wine and sugar. Mix well, simmering about 20 minutes, or until it is smooth. Puree the mixture and return it to the medium-size stainless pan. Simmer until it has reduced by one-half (to about 2 cups). Keep stirring, watching carefully (it easily spatters). It will take about 25 minutes to reduce. Remove from the heat and add the remaining 1/2 cup soft butter, stirring until smooth.

To Serve: Set the marinated pork in a ovenproof pan and add water to just cover the bottom of the pan. Broil about 8" from the heat until done, for approximately 5 minutes, depending on the thickness of the pork. Heat the cranberry wine sauce gently and spoon about 1/4 cup on each plate. Set 4 slices of pork on top of the sauce and serve.

SAVORY PARMESAN GREEN BEANS

SERVES SIX TO EIGHT

Actually, I think my son discovered this recipe a long time ago. I know he liked to make it. It is quick and easy, and has that extra zip that green beans sometimes need. You may use fresh or frozen beans. Half of the cheese is added while cooking and the remaining half is added when the dish is finished, which gives it a nice chewiness.

1/4 cup	Olive oil
4 TB	Chopped onions
1-2 cloves	Garlic, minced
1 1/2 lbs	Green beans, lightly cooked
1 tsp	Salt
1 tsp	Dried basil
1/2 cup	Grated Parmesan

Heat the oil in a large skillet and add the onions and garlic. Sauté for 3-4 minutes over low heat, or until onions are softened. Add the beans, salt and basil. Heat until warm, stirring occasionally. Add one--half of the cheese, stirring to incorporate. Remove from the heat and add the remaining cheese. Taste for seasoning. Serve.

WILD RICE/BASMATI PILAF

SERVES EIGHT

Basmati rice is sort of the Cadillac of white rices. You can certainly substitute any white rice, but basmati will give a richer depth of flavor and character. This pilaf will go together quickly if you have some cooked wild rice on hand.

2 TB	Butter
1/2 cup	Finely chopped onions
1 1/2 cups	Basmati rice
4 cups	Chicken broth
2 tsp	Salt
2 cups	Cooked wild rice, (see page 60)*

In a heavy two quart saucepan with a tight fitting lid, melt the butter over medium-low heat. Add the onions and saute for 3-5 minutes, or until soft and tender. Add the rice, stirring until coated with the butter. In medium size saucepan, bring the chicken broth to a boil. Add the hot broth and salt to the rice. Cover and turn heat to low. Cook for 15 minutes. Turn the heat off. Do not remove the cover for 10 minutes. Gently stir in the wild rice and serve.

CHOCOLATE TORTE

SERVES SIXTEEN

It looks beautiful. The taste is dreamy. We have changed the chocolate cake recipe for the Torte through the years. Originally Suzie Wallace's recipe was used, and now we are using a recipe from the Cafe Beaujolais cookbook. I have changed the recipe slightly. At the Lodge we use Callebaut Belgian chocolate, giving the Torte a rich flavor. Never fear, you can use any chocolate in this recipe and still end up with a wonderful cake.

PREHEAT THE OVEN TO 350 DEGREES.
GREASE TWO 9 INCH ROUND CAKE PANS.

4 oz	Bittersweet chocolate, chopped into small pieces	2 cups	All-purpose Flour
		2 tsp	Baking soda
1/2 cup	Butter, room temperature	1/2 tsp	Salt
2 1/4 cups	Brown sugar	1 cup	Sour cream
3 large	Eggs	1 cup	Coffee, strong
2 tsp	Vanilla		Chocolate Ganache
			Torte Frosting

Melt the chocolate in a microwave or over a double boiler. Let cool. In a mixing bowl, beat the butter and brown sugar until creamy. Add the eggs, beating until light and fluffy (for 5 minutes!). Beat in the cooled chocolate and vanilla. In a separate bowl sift the flour, soda and salt together. Stir in one half of the dry ingredients, one-half of the sour cream, the remaining dry ingredients, and the rest of the sour cream. Stir just until mixed. Gently stir in the coffee. Pour into prepared pans, filling three-fourths full. Drop the pans onto the countertop from a 6 inch height to release air bubbles. Bake at 350 degrees for 35 minutes. Cool 15 minutes on wire racks. Remove from pans.

When the cakes are completely cooled, prepare the Chocolate Ganache.(see next page. Carefully cut each cake in half, so there will be a total of four layers. Spread a thin layer of ganache on the top of each layer, but do not stack them yet. Prepare the Torte Frosting and Filling (see next page).

CHOCOLATE GANACHE

Chocolate Ganache covers each cake layer and creates a base for the frosting and adds extra flavor to the Torte. It is worth this extra touch.

1 cup	Heavy cream
8 oz	semi-sweet chocolate, chopped coarse.

Heat the cream and chocolate in a double boiler until the chocolate is melted, mixing well. Remove from heat and cool slightly. Spread onto each layer.

TORTE FROSTING AND FILLING
A McClanahan family recipe given to Naniboujou.

8 oz	Cream cheese, room temperature
1/2 cup	Brown sugar
1 TB	Vanilla
2 cups	Heavy cream, whipped

In a mixing bowl, beat together the cream cheese, brown sugar and vanilla until fluffy. Fold in the whipped cream, a little at a time. Spread frosting on the top of the ganache, dividing the frosting evenly between layers and saving some for the top. Do not frost sides. Refrigerate until served.

CREAM CHEESE TOMATO SOUP

SERVES EIGHT

This soup was popular when I began my tenure as executive chef. When I read the recipe calling for cans of tomato soup, I did not want to use it. My purist attitude quickly vanished one day. We needed a soup fast!! This soup goes together quickly, so we made a large batch. The customers raved about it. Therefore, it remains one of our main-stays. And gosh, I really like it.

2 TB	Butter	3 cups	Milk
1/2 cup	Finely diced onions	2 cans (14 oz each)	Diced tomatoes
6 ozs	Cream cheese	2 tsp	Basil
2 cans (11 oz each)	Tomato soup	1 TB	Chopped fresh parsley

Melt the butter in a medium saucepan and gently saute the onions until tender, approximately 3-5 minutes. Add the cream cheese, stirring while it melts. Do not let it burn. Mix in the tomato soup until smooth. Turn off the heat. Add the milk slowly, mixing well. Return to heat to continue cooking. Add the diced tomatoes (juice and all) and the basil. Stir and heat until hot. Add parsley, or sprinkle the parsley on top of each bowl when serving.

VEGETARIAN SHEPHERDS PIE

SERVES SIX

Always on the outlook for a vegetarian dish, and again, ways to use left-over mashed potatoes, I improvised this dish that seems to accomplish both. Fortunately, it is also mighty tasty and is filled with a large variety of fresh sauteed vegetables, with a tiny bit of sesame oil for extra flavor. The portions look huge, but it is the "meat", potatoes, and vegetable all rolled into one. We serve it with a simple side dish of pickled beets.

PREHEAT OVEN TO 350 DEGREES.
GREASE A 9 INCH PIE TIN.

POTATO MIXTURE:

5 large	Eggs
9 cups	Mashed potatoes
1 cup	Diced onions
1/4 cup	Butter, melted
1/2 cup	Flour
	Salt and pepper, to taste

VEGGIE MIX:

1/2 cup	Butter
4 cups	Sliced onions
2 1/2 cups	Diced red and yellow peppers, combined
1 cup	Diced green pepper
1 lb	Sliced mushrooms
2 cups	Thinly sliced carrots
6 cloves	Garlic, minced
4 tsp	Dried tarragon
1 TB	Salt
2 tsp	Black pepper
1 tsp	Toasted sesame oil
1/2 cup	Grated Parmesan cheese

POTATO MIXTURE:

In a very large bowl beat the eggs, add the potatoes, onions, butter, flour, and seasonings Mix together and set aside.

VEGGIE MIXTURE:

Melt the butter in a large pan and sauté the onions, peppers, mushrooms, carrots and garlic until tender. Stir occasionally. Do not over-cook or the veggies will get mushy. Remove from the heat and add the tarragon, salt, pepper and sesame oil. Mix well.

Pat one half of the potato mixture on the bottom of the prepared pie pan. Fill it about half full. Flatten with your fingers, so it is level. Mound the veggies (drain if some liquid has accumulated) on top of the potato mixture. There are a lot of veggies to mound up (it resembles a small mountain). Gently mound and press the remaining half of the potato mixture on top of the veggies. Sprinkle the top with Parmesan cheese. Bake for approximately 30 minutes, or until golden brown.

PICKLED BEETS

Of course, you can just buy some canned pickled beets, but this is so simple, and more flavorful.

2 cups	Sugar
1 cup	Cider vinegar
2 cans/11 oz	Whole beets, drained

In a small saucepan, combine the sugar and vinegar. Heat just until the sugar is dissolved. Do not over-cook. Add the drained beets. Refrigerate. We serve about 4-5 small whole beets per person.

CRANBERRY PUDDING WITH HARD SAUCE

SERVES TWELVE TO SIXTEEN

An ultimate comfort food, steamed hot pudding full of rosy cranberries. Nancy has prepared this often for our Christmas caroling dinner dessert, but it is a great dessert any time of the year. Harvey and Lois Turner, dear friends and faithful customers, were kind enough to share this recipe with us.

GENEROUSLY BUTTER A 4-6 CUP MOLD.

2 1/4 cups	Flour	3/4 cup	Light molasses
3/4 cup	Hot water	3/4 cup	Currants, or raisins
3/4 tsp.	Baking soda	3 cups	Coarsely chopped cranberries

Dissolve the flour, water and soda together. Add the molasses, currants and cranberries and pour into the prepared mold. In a large pot with a tight fitting lid pour 2 inches of boiling water into the bottom and set a wire rack, or metal lids to set the mold on. Place mold on the rack and cover the pot tightly. Bring the water to a boil again, lower heat and steam for 35-45 minutes, or until a toothpick inserted in the center comes out clean. Serve with Hard Sauce.

HARD SAUCE

1/2 cup	Butter	1 cup	Heavy cream
1 cup	Sugar	1 TB	Rum

In a small sauce pan, melt the butter over low heat. Mix in the sugar and cream. Heat slowly, bringing to a boil. Immediately remove from heat. Add the rum. Serve warm.

AFTERNOON TEA

FULL MENU:
CUCUMBER CREAM CHEESE SANDWICH
WHITE CHOCOLATE SCONES
with RASPBERRY JAM and WHIPPED CREAM

SWEET BREAD OF THE DAY-(POPPY ALMOND TEA BREAD)
COOKIE OF THE DAY-(SOUR CREAM/NUTMEG COOKIE)
SMOKED TURKEY/DATE FINGER SANDWICH

FRESH STRAWBERRY
BOTTOMLESS POT OF ASHBY'S AFTERNOON TEA

WHITE CHOCOLATE SCONES

MAKES ONE DOZEN

Sweets for the sweet. I have tried to wean our local tea drinkers from these non-traditional sweet scones towards the more typical savory currant scone. No way! This scone recipe is all we ever use anymore. Try them and you will understand.

PREHEAT THE OVEN TO 400 DEGREES.
LIGHTLY GREASE A FLAT BAKING SHEET PAN.

2 cups	Flour
2 TB	Sugar
2 tsp	Baking powder
1/2 tsp	Baking soda
1/2 tsp	Salt
1/4 cup	Butter, cold,
1 large	Egg
2/3 cup	Buttermilk
4-6 ozs	White chocolate chips
	Raspberry jam and whipped cream.

In a large bowl, combine the dry ingredients together. Cut the butter into small pieces and cut butter into the flour mixture with a pastry cutter, or a fork, until evenly incorporated. In a separate bowl, beat the egg and buttermilk together and stir lightly into the flour mixture. Mix in the white chocolate chips. Knead dough together, just until mixed. This is a fairly wet dough-do not add too much flour or handle too much, the scones get tough. On a lightly floured flat surface, pat or roll the dough out to about 1 inch thick. Cut with a round 2 inch floured cookie cutter. Bake approximately 15 minutes, or until a light golden brown on the top. Serve with jam and whipped cream.

POPPYSEED ALMOND TEA BREAD

MAKES TWO LOAVES

PREHEAT THE OVEN TO 350 DEGREES.
GREASE WELL 2 - 4 X 8 INCH LOAF PANS

1 cup	Butter, room temp.	TOPPING	
2 cups	Sugar	1/2 cup	Powdered sugar
3 large	Eggs	2 TB	Orange juice
1 1/2 TB	Poppy seeds	1/2 tsp	Almond flavoring
1 1/2 tsp	Almond extract	1/2 tsp	Vanilla
1 1/2 tsp	Vanilla		
3 cups	Flour		
1 1/2 tsp	Baking powder		
1 tsp	Salt		
1 1/2 cups	Milk		

In a large mixing bowl, cream the butter and sugar until light and fluffy. Add the eggs, continuing to beat after each egg is added. Mix in the poppy seeds, almond extract and vanilla. In a separate bowl, mix the flour, baking powder and salt together. Add these dry ingredients alternately with the milk into the butter mixture. Mix just until thoroughly combined. Pour into prepared pans. Bake approximately 40-45 minutes. Set on a wire rack to cool.

Prepare the topping after you remove the loaves from the oven. Mix the powdered sugar and orange juice together and micro wave for about 30 seconds, or until the sugar is dissolved. Stir in the flavorings. Spoon the warm topping over the warm baked loaves. Continue to cool on wire racks for 10 minutes before removing from pans.

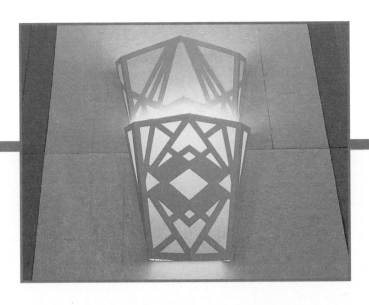

Sour Cream Nutmeg Cookies

Makes five dozen

Our bakers can make anything look great. These tiny free hand drop cookies are a bit more of a challenge for me. This makes a good old fashioned cookie. Check often when baking, they bake up quickly.

PREHEAT THE OVEN TO 350 DEGREES
LIGHTLY GREASE A FLAT BAKING SHEET

1/2 cup	Butter, room temperature
1 cup	Brown sugar
1 large	Egg
1/2 cup	Sour cream
1 cup	All purpose flour
1 cup	Cake flour
2 tsp	Baking powder
1/2 tsp	Baking soda
1/2 tsp	Salt
1/2 tsp	Nutmeg
1 cup	Chopped pecans

In a large mixing bowl, beat the butter and brown sugar together until creamy. Add the egg and sour cream, beating well. Mix the dry ingredients together in a separate bowl and add to the butter mixture, mixing well. Stir in the pecans. Drop by rounded teaspoonful onto the prepared baking sheet pan. Bake 8-10 minutes. Cool on wire racks.

SMOKED TURKEY/DATE FINGER SANDWICH

MAKES 24 TEA SANDWICHES

These finger sandwiches are a fairly new addition to our tea selection. They are pretty and quite tasty. Serve one or two of these triangles on each tea plate.

1 lb	Smoked turkey, diced
1 cup	Butter, room temperature
2 TB	Dijon mustard
4 tsp	Worcheshire sauce
4 tsp	Lemon juice
1 1/4 cup	Fresh parsley, minced
1/3 cup	Chopped green onions
1/2 lb	Dates, pitted and chopped
1/4 tsp	Salt
1/8 tsp	Pepper
6 slices	Whole wheat bread
3/4 cup	Butter, melted

In a food processor, or using an electric mixer, process the turkey, butter, mustard, Worcheshire sauce and lemon juice until smooth. Transfer to a large bowl. Add one-half of the parsley,(save the other half for the sides of the sandwiches), the green onions, dates, salt and pepper. Mix well. Cover, and refrigerate.

TO SERVE: Remove from the refrigerator about 30 minutes before using. Spread the filling on one slice of bread, cover with another slice. Cut off the crusts and cut from corner to corner so you have 4 triangle sandwiches. Dip the edges of each triangle first in the melted butter, then into the remaining parsley. Serve

SUNDAY BRUNCH

At the peak of our tourist season, we serve Sunday Brunch to approximately 200 to 400 people. It is a breakfast buffet. Everything is homemade and fresh. The chafing dishes are piled high with creamy scrambled eggs, breakfast potatoes, crisp bacon, a weekly special breakfast casserole, sweet bread pudding with sour cream rum sauce, plus locally made wild rice/turkey sausage. Bowls and platters of fresh fruits and sliced cheese, yogurt, granola, coffee cake and muffins fill the tables. Belgian waffles are prepared on the spot, accompanied with orange rum syrup. No wonder we are busy.

NANCY'S SOUR CREAM COFFEE CAKE

PEACH MUFFINS

BACON *and* WILD RICE EGG CASSEROLE

SOUTHERN SWEET POTATO BAKE

SWEET BREAD PUDDING *with* SOUR CREAM RUM SAUCE

COCONUT COFFEE CAKE *with* APPLES

LEMON YOGURT MUFFINS

STUFFED BAKED FRENCH TOAST

HAM AND CHEESE POTATO GRATIN

NANCY'S SOUR CREAM COFFEE CAKE

SERVES TWELVE

We prepare this coffee cake often. You can change it using different fruits and nuts. It is a heavy cake, quite moist and full of flavor.

I remember the day that Nancy first made this cake, long ago, when I was working as the morning prep cook. She was singing, as usual, preparing some of her breads over in the baking area. "Let's see," she said, "I think I'll just mix up some butter, add about twice that amount of sugar, a couple of eggs, and of course, flour, baking powder and salt, and maybe a little sour cream and vanilla. Top it off with apple slices, pecans, with a sprinkling of sugar and cinnamon." She had no idea what a winner she created.

PREHEAT THE OVEN TO 350 DEGREES.
GREASE AND FLOUR A 9 X 12 INCH BAKING PAN.

1 cup	Butter	TOPPING:		
2 cups	Sugar	4 cups	Sliced apples, peaches, or blueberries
2 large	Eggs		
2 cups	Flour	1 cup	Chopped pecans
1 tsp	Baking powder	1 tsp	Cinnamon
1/4 tsp	Salt	1/4 cup	Sugar
1 cup	Sour cream		
1/2 tsp	Vanilla		

In a large mixing bowl beat the butter and sugar together until fluffy. Add the eggs, mixing well. In a separate bowl, mix the flour, baking powder and salt together. Gradually add to the butter-sugar mixture, mixing well. Gently mix in the sour cream and vanilla. Spread into the prepared pan. Top with the apples or other fruit and sprinkle on the nuts. Mix the cinnamon and sugar together and dust on top.

Bake for approximately 50-60 minutes, or until a toothpick inserted in the center comes out clean.

PEACH MUFFINS

MAKES 18 MUFFINS

Joy Moneta, above, prepares waffles and also these tender, light muffins, as Naniboujou's Brunch chef. This is a master muffin recipe that we use to make various varieties of fruit muffins—raspberry, strawberry, apple or banana. Just by changing the fruit, and/or the flavoring, you can improvise quite a bit.

PREHEAT THE OVEN TO 350 DEGREES.
GREASE MUFFIN TINS.

3 cups	Flour
1 TB	Baking powder
1/2 tsp	Baking soda
1/2 tsp	Salt
10 TB	Butter, room temperature
1 cup	Sugar
2 large	Eggs
1 tsp	Almond extract
1 1/2 cups	Plain low fat yogurt
1 can 15 oz	Peach slices, drained and cut into small pieces

In a medium-sized bowl, mix the flour, baking powder, baking soda and salt together. In a large mixing bowl, beat the butter and sugar until fluffy. Add the eggs, one at a time, mixing after each addition. Mix in the almond extract. Add half of the dry ingredients and half of the yogurt. Stir just to blend. Gently stir in the remaining dry ingredients and the yogurt. Add the peaches. Do not over-mix. Fill the prepared muffin tins 2/3 full. Bake approximately 15-20 minutes, or until a toothpick inserted in center comes out clean.

Bacon and Wild Rice Casserole

Serves Six to Eight

Just a little bit of the right things creates this memorable breakfast entree. It looks interesting, so most people want to give it a try, and they do come back for more. We bake this casserole in large quantities trying to keep up with the crowd's appetite.

Preheat the oven to 350 degrees.
Grease a 8 x 12 inch baking dish.

8 ozs	Sliced bacon	1/2 cup	Grated Swiss cheese
1 TB	Butter	1/2 cup	Grated Cheddar cheese
8 ozs	Sliced fresh mushrooms	2 TB	Chopped fresh parsley
1/2 cup	Diced green onions	1 TB	Dried tarragon
1/2 cup	Diced red peppers	1 tsp	Grated nutmeg
9 large	Eggs	1 tsp	Salt
1 1/4 cups	Half-and-half	1 tsp	Pepper
3/4 cup	Wild rice, cooked		

In a large skillet, sauté the bacon until crisp. Drain the bacon on paper towels. Save the drippings. Crumble or chop the bacon and set it aside. Use some of the dripping with the butter to saute the mushrooms, green onions and red peppers until most of their liquid has evaporated.

In a large mixing bowl, beat the eggs and add the half-and-half and mix well. Mix in the bacon, vegetables, wild rice, cheeses, herbs, salt and pepper combining everything together thoroughly. Pour this mixture into the prepared baking dish. Bake for approximately 45 minutes, or until a knife inserted in the center comes out clean.

SOUTHERN SWEET POTATO BAKE

SERVES TWELVE

Sweet potatoes for breakfast? People love to see this dish on the buffet. They find room on overflowing plates for a bright dollop of this southern dish to accompany their sausage, eggs, muffin and fruit.

PREHEAT THE OVEN TO 325 DEGREES.
BUTTER A 8 X 12 INCH PAN.

8	Sweet potatoes
1 large	Egg, lightly beaten
1 can (8oz)	Crushed pineapple, drained
1/2 cup	Brown sugar
1/2 cup	Butter, melted
2 TB	Grated orange peel
1 tsp	Salt
1 tsp	Cinnamon
1 tsp	Vanilla

Peel and cut the sweet potatoes into large chunks. Put them into a large kettle and cover with water. Bring to a boil, turn heat down and simmer until the potatoes are soft, but not mushy. Drain. Mash the potatoes in a large mixing bowl. Add the remining ingredients, and mix well. Scoop the mixture into the prepared pan and level off. Bake approximately 30 minutes, or until set.

VARIATION: Sprinkle top with chopped toasted pecans before baking.

SWEET BREAD PUDDING

SERVES TWELVE TO SIXTEEN

Naniboujou is noted by local residents for its Sweet Bread Pudding served every week at the Sunday brunch. Some come just for this special morning dessert. And, who knows how many are also addicted to the Sour Cream Rum Sauce we prepare to top it off. The difficulty in reproducing this recipe is that each week it is actually a different pudding. We use our left-over muffins mixed with a little bread for each pan. Since we're always making different muffins, one Sunday you may be eating an oatmeal, blueberry and lemon yogurt muffin pudding, and the next Sunday a pan of banana pecan chocolate chip and raspberry muffin bread pudding. At home you too can improvise—any good left over muffin, or bread, or even cinnamon rolls will do the trick.

PREHEAT THE OVEN TO 300 DEGREES.

GREASE AN 8 X 12 INCH BAKING PAN.

8 cups	Muffins and bread, cut into 1 1/2 inch chunks
9 large	Eggs
1/2 cup	Sugar
2 cups	Half and half
4 cups	Milk
	Sour Cream Rum Sauce

Fill the pan about 1/2 full with the muffin-bread mixture. In a large mixing bowl, beat the eggs. Add the sugar, half-and-half and milk and mix well. Pour this mixture over the dry bread mixture filling the pan 3/4 full. Bake on lower oven rack for approximately 1 hour and 15 minutes, or until set. It should be lightly browned and not jiggle in the middle. To check if done, insert a knife into the middle of the pudding. It should come out fairly clean.

Serve warm with Sour Cream Rum Sauce.

SOUR CREAM RUM SAUCE

MAKES 4 CUPS

How can something so simple taste so good? Look at the ingredients—sour cream, sugar, rum. Hmmm, no more questions. Serve this over bread pudding, waffles, or cakes. Just remember—a little goes a long way.

16 oz	Sour cream
3/4 cup	Sugar
1/3 cup	Rum
3 TB	Water

In a small saucepan, over low heat, mix the sour cream and sugar. Mix in the rum and water. Heat and serve warm.

Coconut Coffee Cake with Apples

Serves Eight to Twelve

There is nothing like a warm, moist coffee cake on a Sunday morning. You can use other fruits as filling, but I think fresh apple slices sets off this coconut almond cake best. It is a favorite old recipe of mine.

Preheat the oven to 350 degrees.
Grease an 9 x 12 inch baking pan.

1 cup	Butter, room temperature
1 1/2 cups	Sugar
4 large	Eggs
2 1/4 cups	Flour
1 TB	Baking powder
1 1/2 tsp	Baking soda
1/2 tsp	Salt
2/3 cup	Buttermilk
1 tsp	Almond extract
2 cups	Coconut
2 cups	Diced, peeled apples
1/2 cup	Slivered almonds
1/3 cup	Brown sugar
1 1/2 tsp	Cinnamon

In a large mixing bowl, beat the butter and sugar until fluffy. Add the eggs, one at a time, mixing well after each egg is added. In a separate bowl, mix the dry ingredients together and add to the butter mixture, mixing just until combined. Add the buttermilk and the almond extract, mixing until well blended. Fold in the coconut. Spread into the prepared pan. Sprinkle the apples and almonds on top, and then sprinkle the sugar and cinnamon on top. Bake about 25 minutes, or until tooth pick inserted in center comes out clean.

LEMON YOGURT MUFFINS

1 DOZEN

We make a couple of different lemon muffins, but I believe this one is young Kristen Ramey's favorite. When she requested lemon muffins, it took me a while to figure out which one she liked, but she definitely knew. I love to watch her work her way down the buffet line. She doesn't eat much at a time, but she is back often. Simple choices, a pile of scrambled eggs, a lemon yogurt muffin, or Belgian waffles, a huge fresh strawberry, and that's it. These are light muffins, not overly sweet.

PREHEAT THE OVEN TO 375 DEGREES.
GREASE MUFFIN TINS.

2 cups	Flour	1 1/4 cups	Plain yogurt
1 tsp	Baking powder	1/4 cup	Butter, melted
1 tsp	Baking soda	1 TB	Grated lemon peel
1/4 tsp	Salt	SYRUP:	
1/4 cup	Sugar	1/3 cup	Lemon juice
2 TB	Honey	1/3 cup	Sugar
2 large	Eggs, lightly beaten	3 TB	Water

In a mixing bowl, combine the flour, baking powder, baking soda and salt. In a separate large mixing bowl, combine the sugar, honey, eggs, yogurt, melted butter and lemon peel. Beat until well mixed.

Add the dry ingredients to the mixture, stir only until blended. Fill each muffin cup 2/3 full. Bake for approximately 15 minutes, or until a tooth pick inserted in the center comes out clean.

SYRUP: In a small sauce pan, combine the lemon juice, sugar and water and bring to a boil. Boil 2 minutes. When the muffins are out of the oven, poke each with a fork and liberally drizzle the lemon syrup over the tops. If you like a sweeter muffin, also sprinkle the tops with sugar. Do not remove from the muffin tin for about 5 minutes.

STUFFED BAKED FRENCH TOAST

SERVES EIGHT

Do you want to make everyone happy? Set this golden, chunky baked dish down in the center of the dining room table for a comforting breakfast feast. We serve this not only at the buffet, but also to our Elderhostel folks, who always give this dish rave reviews.

PREHEAT THE OVEN TO 350 DEGREES
BUTTER A 9 X 12 INCH PAN.

1 lb	French bread, cubed
8 ozs	Cream cheese, diced into 1" pcs
8 large	Eggs
2 1/2 cups	Half and half
6 TB	Butter, melted and cooled
1/4 cup	Maple syrup
	Cinnamon

Put one half of the bread cubes in the prepared pan. Spread the cream cheese evenly on top. Add the rest of the bread cubes. In a large mixing bowl, beat the eggs well. Add the half and half, butter and maple syrup. Pour the mixture evenly over the top of the bread. Press the bread down slightly to make sure everything is moistened. Cover with plastic wrap and refrigerate overnight. Sprinkle with a little cinnamon before baking. Bake about 45 minutes, or until golden brown.

HAM AND CHEESE POTATO GRATIN

SERVES SIX TO EIGHT

Potato gratins come in many forms. The wonders of a little garlic and dry mustard for extra flavor plus the basics makes this an easy, tasty dish to prepare.

PREHEAT THE OVEN TO 350 DEGREES

2 TB	Butter
2 qts	Diced, peeled potatoes
3 cloves	Garlic, finely minced
8 oz	Ham, diced
12 oz	Swiss cheese
2 large	Eggs
2 cups	Milk
1 1/2 cups	Half and half
1 TB	Dry mustard
1 1/2 tsp	Salt
3/4 tsp	Black pepper

Butter a 8 x 12 inch baking dish and spread the potatoes evenly in the prepared baking dish. Using a fork, mix the garlic, ham and cheese into the potatoes. In a large bowl mix the eggs, milk, half and half, dry mustard, pepper, salt, and pepper together. Pour this mixture over the top of the potato mixture and gently mix all together. Bake approximately 40 minutes, or until golden brown and set.

ELDERHOSTEL MENU'S

Each spring and autumn we host an Elderhostel group of approximately 45 people. Everything is served buffet style, so I use recipes not normally served in the restaurant. Many of these guests have requested recipes. I hope the following selection will satisfy some of those desires. All in all, I think they eat quite well. We thank them for their gracious appreciation of the facility, staff, and the food.

BREAKFAST:
JUICE, FRUIT, COFFEE *or* TEA
BAKED OATMEAL *with* MAPLE SYRUP
BLUEBERRY SOUR CREAM MUFFINS

LUNCH:
CHICKEN CORN NOODLE SOUP
SLICED CHEESE *and* CRACKERS
FRESH GREEN SALAD WITH HERB VINAIGRETTE
CHOCOLATE CHIP ORANGE SHORT BREAD COOKIES

DINNER:
BAKED FISH *with* MUSTARD CRUMBS
BAKED POTATOES
CORN PUDDING
GINGER PUMPKIN FROST

BLUEBERRY SOUR CREAM MUFFINS

MAKES 18 MUFFINS

Blueberries may grow wild in our local woods, but because of the large quantities we use we must be satisfied purchasing commercial berries from our supplier. If you are able to obtain wild berries, certainly use them. Sour cream gives these muffins extra flavor and moisture.

PREHEAT THE OVEN TO 375
GREASE MUFFIN TINS

10 TB	Butter, room temperature	2 1/2 cups	Flour
1 1/2 cups	Sugar	1 1/2 tsp	Baking powder
2 large	Eggs	3/4 tsp	Baking soda
10 TB	Sour cream	1/4 tsp	Salt
1 1/2 tsp	Vanilla	3/4 cup	Blueberries

In a large mixing bowl, cream the butter and sugar until fluffy. Mix in the eggs, one at a time. Add the sour cream and vanilla, mixing well. In a medium size bowl, mix the flour, baking powder, baking soda and salt together. Stir the dry ingredients into the butter mixture and mix just until blended. Fold in the berries. Fill the muffin tins 2/3 full. Bake for about 12-15 minutes, or until toothpick inserted in the center comes out clean.

BAKED OATMEAL

SERVES SIX

For many years, the Adventurous Christians, located on the Gunflint Trail, have served hundreds or thousands of group meals. This oatmeal dish was provided by one of their cooks. An Elderhostel favorite!

PREHEAT OVEN TO 300 DEGREES.
GREASE AN 8 X 8 INCH BAKING DISH.

3 large	Eggs, lightly beaten	2 tsp	Baking powder
1 3/4 cups	Milk	1 1/4 tsp	Salt
1/2 cup	Corn oil	4 3/4 cups	Oatmeal
1 cup	Brown sugar	1/4 tsp each	Cinnamon and nutmeg

In a small bowl, combine and mix the eggs, milk, and corn oil together. In a large bowl, mix the remaining ingredients, adding the milk mixture. Pour into prepared baking dish. Bake approximately 45 minutes, or until firm. Serve with milk and sugar.

CHICKEN CORN NOODLE

SERVES SIX TO EIGHT

Everyone loves chicken noodle soup. Adding corn gives the soup a little more color and flavor. Also, to make it more interesting, the noodles could be any shape or color you want. Spinach noodles are nice. We usually use linguine noodles that we have on hand, breaking them up into short pieces.

1 1/2 lbs	Chicken breasts, boneless and skinless
6 cups	Water
2 TB	Butter
3/4 cup	Leeks (or onions), diced
1/2 cup	Celery, diced
1 large	Carrot, diced
2 ozs	Dry pasta
1 1/2 tsp	Salt
1 cup	Corn, frozen or fresh
1/2 tsp	Pepper
3/4 tsp	Dried basil
3/4 tsp	Dried thyme
2 TB	Fresh parsley, finely diced

Bring the water to a boil in a large kettle and add the chicken. Lower the heat and simmer about 15 minutes, or until chicken is cooked through. Careful not to overcook. Remove the chicken from the broth and set aside. Save the broth in the kettle. Meanwhile, in a large skillet over low heat, melt the butter and saute the leeks (use only the white of leek) for about 10 minutes or until tender. Add the leeks, celery and carrots to the chicken broth and bring to a boil. Add the pasta noodles and the salt. Cover, and over medium heat cook about 10-12 minutes or until the pasta is done and the veggies are cooked through. Cut the chicken breasts into 1" pieces and add to the soup pot. Add the corn, pepper, basil, thyme and parsley. Heat until hot. Taste for seasoning.

HERB VINAIGRETTE

MAKES 2 CUPS

This is my basic vinaigrette dressing, with the addition of dijon mustard and garlic, which you could leave out if you like a milder dressing. I like the combination of the two oils. Corn oil has so much flavor, but you may use any oil of preference, realizing that it will have a different flavor. Go ahead make a batch. Homemade dressing tastes so much fresher than the bottled dressings. It keeps a long time in the refrigerator. Take it out an hour before serving, if possible, as it will taste and mix up better.

1/2 cup	Red wine vinegar	1 clove	Garlic, minced
2 tsp	Salt	3/4 cup	Corn oil
1/2 tsp	Pepper	3/4 cup	Olive oil
1 TB	Dijon mustard	2 tsp	Dried herbs; mixture of tarragon, thyme and basil

In a small bowl, whisk the vinegar with the salt, until the salt dissolves. Mix in the pepper, mustard and garlic. In another small bowl, mix the oils together with a fork. Slowly whisk the oils into the vinegar mixture. You can pour a little faster after you have incorporated about one fourth of the oil. Whisk continuously until all the oil is incorporated. Mix in the herbs. Let the dressing sit at room temperature before using. Refrigerate.

CHOCOLATE CHIP ORANGE SHORTBREAD COOKIES

MAKES 6 DOZEN

Quick, easy, melt in your mouth, tiny cookies. So good they'll disappear fast.

PREHEAT THE OVEN TO 350 DEGREES.

3/4 cup	Powdered sugar	1	Orange zest (grated peel)
1 1/2 cups	Butter	6 ozs	Mini chocolate chips
3 cups	Flour		

In a large mixing bowl, beat the powdered sugar and butter together. Beat in the flour and orange zest. Fold in the chocolate chips. Roll into 1" balls (about a rounded teaspoon full), and flatten with a cookie stamp, or the bottom of a small glass dipped in flour. Bake on ungreased cookie sheets for approximately 8-10 minutes. Cool on wire racks.

BAKED FISH WITH MUSTARD CRUMBS

SERVES SIX TO EIGHT

If we have no walleye, I substitute cod. This recipe is flexible in that way, but the oven time will vary depending on the thickness of the fish fillets. Your kitchen will smell great after this is popped into the oven.

PREHEAT THE OVEN TO 400 DEGREES.

6 TB	Butter, melted
3 lbs	Walleye, skinned and filleted
4	Shallots, peeled and minced
2 cloves	Garlic, peeled and minced
3/4 cup	Dry white wine
2 TB	Lemon juice
	Salt and pepper
2 cups	Fresh bread crumbs*
2 TB	Dijon mustard
1/2 cup	Minced fresh parsley

Pour the butter into an 9 x 12 inch pan. Lay the fish fillets flat in one layer. Sprinkle the shallots and garlic on the top of the fillets. Mix the white wine and lemon juice together and pour over the fish. Season well. In a small bowl mix the bread crumbs with the Dijon and parsley. Pat, or spread as evenly as possible over the top of the fish. Bake uncovered, approximately 20-25 minutes. The fish should be flaky, yet still moist.

*Process cubes of bread in a food processor or a blender until fine consistency.

CORN PUDDING

SERVES EIGHT

We always use frozen corn and sometimes have difficulty with too much moisture, so by all means use fresh corn, if available. Also, frozen corn requires longer baking time. The pudding will thicken a little after it comes out of the oven and sits for a short time. Gooey or firm, it is a hit.

PREHEAT THE OVEN TO 375 DEGREES.
BUTTER AN 8 X 8 INCH BAKING DISH.

2 large	Eggs
1 1/4 cups	Half and half
1 1/4 cups	Cream
2 TB	Brown sugar
1/2 tsp	Ground nutmeg
2 tsp	Salt
1/2 tsp	Pepper
6 cups	Frozen corn (thawed), or fresh
1/4 cup	Chopped chive
6 leaves	Red cabbage - optional

In a large mixing bowl, beat the eggs well. Add the half and half, cream, brown sugar, nutmeg, salt and pepper, mixing well. Stir in the corn.

Pour into the prepared baking dish. Bake approximately 45 minutes, or until set. Sprinkle with chives when serving. Or, if using the red cabbage leaves, place a leaf on each plate, spoon corn pudding in middle of leaf and sprinkle with chives.

GINGER PUMPKIN FROST

SERVES EIGHT

This is Marcia Stoub's recipe. She has prepared this for groups dining at the Lodge. Many guests request the recipe, so here goes. Because this is a frozen dessert, it is very refreshing. So, do not be afraid to serve pumpkin, even in the middle of the summer.

12	Gingersnaps	1/2 tsp	Cinnamon
1 cup	Canned pumpkin	1/4 tsp	Nutmeg
1/2 cup	Sugar	1/2 cup	Chopped pecans
1/4 tsp	Salt	1 qt	Vanilla ice cream (slightly softened)

Break up about 8 of the gingersnaps into small pieces and sprinkle them over the bottom of a 9″ pie tin. In a large bowl, mix the pumpkin, sugar, salt and spices together, mixing well. Stir in the pecans. Cut the ice cream into about 8 sections, then beat it into the mixture. Spread it all into the pie tin. Chop the remaining 4 gingersnaps into little pieces and sprinkle over the top. Freeze. Cut when ready to serve.

CHRISTMAS CAROLING DINNER

A PAST MENU FROM 1997

MULLED CIDER

SWEET RED PEPPER VELOUTE SOUP

MIXED GREEN SALAD *with*

PECANS, FETA AND CIDER DRESSING

SEARED DUCK BREAST *with* LINGONBERRY BROWN SAUCE

WILD RICE *with* LEEKS

BAKED SWEET POTATO/PEAR COMPOTE

GRATEFUL PUDDING WITH SOUR LEMON SAUCE

MULLED CIDER

SERVES EIGHT TO TEN

Holiday guests are greeted by Nancy and staff as they enter the dining room, then guided past the roaring fireplace and into the bright solarium. There the guests socialize with one another, sipping spicy hot cider until dinner is announced. The Caroling Dinners have been a tradition at Naniboujou since 1985.

2 quarts	Apple cider	1/2 tsp	Whole cloves
1/4 cup	Brown sugar	1/2 tsp	Ground cardamom
2 large	Bay leaves	1/2 tsp	Nutmeg
2 sticks	Cinnamon	1 large	Orange

In a large kettle, combine all the ingredients and bring to a boil. Lower the heat and simmer, uncovered, for 30 minutes. Strain, and discard the spices and orange. Serve warm.

Sweet Red Pepper Veloute Soup

Serves Six to Eight

If a young teenager, such as seventeen year old Paul Ramey, raves about a soup, then I know it is good. Paul, Peter, Arja and Heather Ramey help other staff members set up the dining room for the holiday dinners. They help prep the food, and also graciously serve our holiday guests this traditional, festive repast. It is a two night affair, the same menu each evening, different guests. I have enjoyed planning these special menus.

3 large	Red peppers
1 large	Onion, finely chopped
4 TB	Butter
1 clove	Garlic, minced
pinch	Cayenne powder
3 1/2 cups	Chicken broth, or homemade chicken stock
2 tsp	Lemon juice
2 tsp	Salt
2 1/2 cups	Veloute sauce (recipe below)
1/2 cup	Heavy cream
1 TB	Cognac

Broil the red peppers until the skin turns black. Immediately put them into a paper bag and close. Wait about 10 minutes, then you should be able to peel the skins off the peppers. Discard the skins and seeds and roughly chop the peppers. In a large kettle, melt the butter over medium low heat. Add the peppers, onion and garlic, sauteing until tender. (Do not let the onion brown.) Add the cayenne, chicken broth, lemon juice and salt. Bring to a boil and lower heat. Cover and simmer about 20 minutes. Puree in a blender.

Veloute sauce: Melt 3 tablespoons of butter in a large skillet. Whisk in 3 tablespoons of flour. Continually whisk for about 2 minutes in order for the flour to cook. Gradually whisk in 2 cups of milk. Season with salt and pepper.

Slowly add the soup stock to the veloute sauce, whisking continuously over low heat. Add the cream and cognac. Serve hot.

MIXED GREEN SALAD WITH PECANS, FETA AND CIDER DRESSING

SERVES EIGHT

Sarah Leah Chase inspires me. I slightly revised this recipe from her Cold Weather Cooking cook book. Many of her recipes are rather involved, as this one is, but for a special occasion it is well worth the effort. You will end up with extra spiced pecans to use on future salads. Save them in an airtight container.

PREHEAT THE OVEN TO 300 DEGREES.

SPICED PECANS:

2 cups	Pecan halves
2 1/2 TB	Corn oil
1/4 cup	Sugar
1 tsp	Salt
1 tsp	Ground cinnamon
1/4 tsp	Ground nutmeg
1/4 tsp	Ground cloves
1/2 tsp	Ground ginger
1/2 tsp	Dry mustard

HOT CIDER DRESSING:

2 cups	Apple cider
8 slices	Bacon, cut into 1" pieces
2	Shallots, minced
1 tsp	Ground cinnamon
1 TB	Honey mustard
1/2 cup	Olive oil
	Salt and pepper

GREEN SALAD:

8 cups	Mixed greens
1 large	McIntosh apple, diced
4 ozs	Feta cheese

SPICED PECANS: Put the pecans into a small bowl and cover with boiling water. Soak for 15 minutes, then drain and pat dry. Spread on an ungreased baking sheet and bake, stirring occasionally, for 40 minutes. Remove the nuts. Turn the oven temperature to 350 degrees. Whisk the corn oil, sugar, salt and spices together. Add the hot nuts and toss to coat them thoroughly. Spread again on the baking sheet and toast for about 10 minutes. Watch carefully, they burn easily. Cool.

HOT CIDER DRESSING: In a small saucepan, boil the apple cider until reduced to one-half cup (about 20 minutes). In a skillet, saute the bacon until crisp. Drain on paper towels. Using 3 tablespoons of the bacon fat, saute the shallots in the skillet until tender. Whisk in the cinnamon and mustard. Add the cider and olive oil.

TO SERVE: Toss the greens with 1 cup of the pecans, bacon, apple and feta. Add the hot cider dressing and toss. Serve immediately.

SEARED DUCK BREAST WITH LINGONBERRY BROWN SAUCE

SERVES EIGHT

The holidays are filled with traditional foods. I wanted to serve an entree that was special and different, yet appealing to most appetites. The simplicity of this dish makes it easy to do at home. Lingonberries might be the problem. Scandinavian stores carry the preserves. A raspberry or blueberry preserve would be a fine substitute.

4	Duck breasts/ cut in half

MARINADE:

2 cups	Peach nectar, or drained juice from canned peaches
2 TB	Thyme
2 cups	Red wine

LINGONBERRY BROWN SAUCE:

	Juices from searing the duck breasts
3/4 cup	Raspberry vinegar
3/4 cup	Lingonberry preserves
1 cup	Heavy cream

MARINADE: Mix the nectar, thyme and red wine together. Put the 8 pieces of duck breast in a flat dish. Cover with marinade and refrigerate for 1-3 hours. Heat two heavy skillets (cast iron if possible). Remove duck from the marinade and sear the breasts, about 3-4 minutes per side. (Duck is supposed to be served rather pink in the middle, but cook longer if desired.) Save the skillets unwashed to prepare the lingonberry brown sauce. Set the seared breasts into an ovenproof dish, cover with foil and set into low oven (200 degree) to keep warm.

LINGONBERRY BROWN SAUCE: Divide the sauce ingredients between the two skillets. First add the raspberry vinegar to each skillet. Over medium heat, scrape each skillet to loosen the bits of duck off the bottom, using a fork or a whisk. Add the lingonberry preserves and mix well. Pour in cream, mixing and heating until hot. To serve; drizzle the sauce over each duck breast.

WILD RICE AND LEEKS

Serves Six to Eight

Wild rice and leeks are both special ingredients. This dish is a great accompaniment to any entree, but especially nice with poultry.

4 TB	Butter
5 small	Leeks, chopped, white only
1 1/2 cups	Wild rice
3 cups	Chicken broth
3/4 tsp	Salt
3/4 tsp	Pepper
1/2 cup	Sliced almonds, toasted*

In a 2 quart kettle, melt the butter over low heat and add the leeks. Sauté for about 3-5 minutes. Add the rice, stock, salt and pepper and bring to a boil. Lower heat, cover and simmer 30 minutes or more, or until rice is cooked.

In a hot, dry skillet heat the sliced almonds for a couple of minutes, stirring constantly until the almonds begin to slightly brown. Remove immediately from the heat. Serve the rice sprinkled with almonds.

Sweet Potato and Pear Compote
Serves *Eight*

A wonderful combination. A revised recipe from the *Open House Cookbook*. You can prepare this dish the day before serving and simply reheat it in the oven for about 10-15 minutes.

PREHEAT THE OVEN TO 375 DEGREES.
BUTTER AN 9 X 12 INCH BAKING DISH.

4 large	Sweet potatoes, peeled and sliced into 1/2" slices
4 large	Ripe pears, peeled, cored and cut lengthwise into 8 pieces per pear
1/2 cup	Brandy
1/3 cup	Orange juice
1/2 cup	Packed brown sugar
3 TB	Butter
1/2 cup	Golden raisins
3/4 tsp	Salt

In a medium saucepan, cover the sweet potato slices with water and heat to boiling. Lower heat and simmer uncovered until barely tender, about 12 minutes or less. Drain well.

Layer the sweet potato slices and the pear pieces together in the prepared baking dish. In a small saucepan, combine the brandy, orange juice, brown sugar, and butter. Heat over medium heat until the sugar is dissolved and the butter melted. Add the raisins and salt and pour over the sweet potatoes and pears. Stir to distribute evenly. Bake until browned and bubbly, approximately 45 minutes.

GRATEFUL PUDDING WITH SOUR LEMON SAUCE

SERVES EIGHT

I am eternally grateful for this Martha Stewart recipe. I have converted it from a steamed pudding to a baked lemony bread pudding. Indeed, a happy ending to a holiday meal.

PUDDING:

1/4 cup	Golden raisins
1/4 cup	Currants
1/4 cup	Cognac
1	Lemon peel, grated
4 cups	French bread, crusts removed, cut into 1" pieces
3 cups	Cinnamon bread, crusts removed, cut into 1" pieces
2 cups	Heavy cream
4 large	Eggs
2/3 cup	Sugar
1 1/2 tsp	Vanilla
1/2 tsp	Mace

SOUR LEMON SAUCE:

3/4 cup	Sugar
1 1/2 TB	Cornstarch
1/8 tsp	Salt
1 1/4 cups	Hot water
3 1/2 TB	Butter
4 TB	Lemon juice
4 tsp	Grated lemon peel

Soak the raisins and currants in the cognac overnight. Preheat oven to 350°. Butter an 9 x 12 inch baking dish and sprinkle a little sugar evenly over bottom of the dish. Layer the breads alternately with the raisin/currant mix. In a small saucepan, scald the cream, and then cool slightly. In a mixing bowl, beat the egg and add the sugar, mixing until light. Gradually pour and mix in the scalded cream, adding the vanilla and mace. Pour over the bread mix. Set a pan of hot water in the bottom of the oven and set the bread pudding on the oven rack above it. Bake until golden brown and firm, approximately40-45 minutes.

SOUR LEMON SAUCE: In a double boiler combine the sugar, cornstarch and salt. Add the hot water and stir, cooking until thickened. Add the butter, lemon juice and lemon peel. Continue to stir, cooking until smooth. Serve the warm sauce over the baked pudding.

ACKNOWLEDGEMENTS AND NOTES FROM THE CHEF

"It seems to me that our three basic needs,
for food and security and love, are so mixed
and mingled and entwined that we cannot
straightly think of one without the other."

M.F.K. Fisher
The Gastronomical Me

Food is my passion. Whether cooking, eating, reading or writing about it, food gives me abundant pleasure. This cookbook gives me the opportunity to share that joy by providing recipes that have become important to our guests. Cooking is a labor of love, and, I have discovered, so is writing a cookbook.

I would like to express my gratitude to Tim and Nancy for their unbelievable confidence, support and love. I appreciate the time and effort my husband, Richard, and my daughter, Lynn, have given to help with editing, along with my friends, Ann Mershon and Joan Crosby. Family, friends and staff members have also done a lot of tasting and critiquing. Many of our recipes were for large quantities, so even though they worked well at the restaurant, I did have to break them down to family proportions. Last, but certainly not least, I thank my predecessor, Kevin Streeter, for establishing high culinary standards during his lengthy tenure at Naniboujou.

I was eager to carry on these standards when I arrived in 1996. Again, Tim and Nancy gave me complete support and free rein to create my own specialties. I was a neighbor and friend of the Rameys, so they were familiar with my background. They watched me through my years of homesteading on an old Hovland farm, with Nubian goat milk, fresh eggs, and garden produce to create meals for my family, to a later shift of my energies toward developing a small pizza restaurant in Grand Marais. Pierre's Pizza actually began with the help of Nancy, who gave me advice and assistance from her experience with her own family's pizza business.

Developing Pierre's recipes was not enough. I was determined to learn and do more, which led me to study at the French cooking school, LaVarenne, in Paris, France. This was followed by a new business enterprise in Stillwater, Minnesota. My daughter Lynn and I created a small cafe/deli, A Little Lunch. We labored long and hard producing abundant homemade baked goods, soups, salads, sandwiches and desserts.

Later, I began giving a few cooking classes, writing a food column for the local newspaper and feeding friends and family.

I have often wondered, where did this passion of mine come from? Did the spark come from that toy electric stove I received one Christmas morning long ago? Or was it my maternal grandmother's house, which was filled with the smells of yeast bread puffing roundly in a large ceramic bowl, dozens of crisp sugar cookies cooling, and often, a platter of golden fried chicken sitting for the taking?

A neighbor, Mrs. Bottacavola, actually gave me my first recipe. At fifteen I was determined to learn her method of producing wonderful, robust tomato sauce, which she brewed all day long every Monday. She did not hand me a recipe card. I watched and took notes. Years later, what I learned from her allowed me to create my Pierre's pizza sauce.

Many cooks have inspired me, and many food writers. Yet, my passion is quite personal. I believe that food is an important, basic need. The quality, the quantity, the preparation, the presentation, all affect our physical, emotional and psychological well being. I hope at Naniboujou Lodge I have passed on to our staff this love of producing good food. And, to our diners, I hope to pass on the enjoyment of a meal created with love and attention.

My present source of inspiration comes from seeing the sparkle in the eyes of my grand children, as they don an apron, pull up a chair, climb up by my side and stir their love into a bowl.

"Food, security and love all mingled and entwined."

Bonnie Jean Swanson

INDEX